AUGUST & SEPTEMBER

Make the Most of Every Month with Carson-Dellosa's Monthly Books!

Production Manager
Chris McIntyre

Editorial Director
Jennifer Weaver-Spencer

Writers
Lynette Pyne
Amy Gamble
Lynn Ruppard
Karen M. Smith

Editors
Kelly Gunzenhauser
Maria McKinney
Carol Layton

Art Director
Penny Casto

Art Coordinator
Edward Fields

Carson-Dellosa Art Adaptations
Mike Duggins
Erik Huffine
David Lackey
Ray Lambert
Betsy Peninger
J.J. Rudisill
Pam Thayer
Todd Tyson
Julie Webb

Cover Design
Amber Kocher Crouch
Ray Lambert
J.J. Rudisill

Carson-Dellosa Publishing Company, Inc.

Table of Contents

AUGUST/SEPTEMBER TEACHER TIPS

Memory Book

Plan to keep a class memory book as a keepsake of the school year. Use poster board to make a front and back cover and inside pages. Take photos of different classroom events throughout the year and glue them in the book. Have students write about the events and include these in the book as well. At the end of the school year, have each student sign his name on the last page of the book. Share past memory books with new classes.

Parent Folders

Use parent folders to keep parents informed of their child's activities throughout the year. Provide a folder containing two pockets for each child. Label the outside of the folder with the child's name. Label the left pocket *Things to Keep* and the right pocket *Things to Return*. Send important papers home in these folders so parents will know at a glance what information they can keep and what information they need to complete and send back to you.

Storage Containers

Students can make their own decorative containers to hold school supplies. Collect cylinder-shaped potato chip canisters with lids. Cover the cans with decorative self-adhesive paper. Write each student's name on a canister. Fill the canisters with school supplies, such as crayons, pencils, erasers, and scissors. Students can store their canisters inside their desks.

Collecting Materials

Stock up for a creative year! Begin gathering craft and project materials at the beginning of the school year so you will have the things you need on hand. Plan ahead and make a list of recyclable items such as cardboard tubes, cereal boxes, and egg cartons and send it home with students. Have a designated place where students can place the materials they bring in.

Everybody Line Up!

Avoid confusion while students are lining up by placing pieces of colored masking tape indicating where students should stand on the classroom floor or carpet. Space apart the tape markers so students are far enough apart. Label the first piece of tape with a permanent marker to indicate where the line leader should stand.

Classroom Stationery

Have students help you make customized classroom stationery to use for writing notes and reminders to send home. On white paper, have each student decorate a frame around the border of the page. Use these pages as stationery to send letters to parents during the year.

August Day-by-Day Calendar

1 *Francis Scott Key's Birthday* Born in 1779, he wrote our national anthem, *The Star Spangled Banner*. Play it and discuss what the lyrics mean.

2 *National Clown Week* is the first full week in August. Give each child a paper plate and have him draw a clown face on it. Glue yarn around the edge for hair.

3 *Columbus set sail from Spain* on this day in 1492. Have students come up with headlines that might have appeared when Columbus reached land.

4 *Louis Armstrong's Birthday* He was born in 1901. Share some of this jazz great's music with the class.

5 *Neil Armstrong's Birthday* Born in 1930, this astronaut was the first person to walk on the moon. Due to less gravity, weight on the moon is $\frac{1}{6}$ of what it is on Earth. Using calculators, let students find their moon weights.

6 *National Fresh Breath Day* Share gum or mints with the class to celebrate.

7 *Sandwich Month* Bring in bread, spreads, and meats and celebrate sandwiches!

8 *Jaqueline Cochrane* was the *first woman to break the sound barrier*. She did it on this day in 1980 at the age of 80. Have students write or tell about what they imagine they will do when they are 80.

9 *Smokey Bear's Birthday* He was "born" in 1950. Make a class list of campfire safety rules. Then, make campfire safety booklets illustrating these rules.

10 *Smithsonian Institution was founded* on this day in 1846. Have students brainstorm a list of museums they would like to see at the Smithsonian. If they could add one, what would it be? Would there be a museum dedicated to dogs? Comic book heroes? A favorite food?

11 *National Parks Month* Have students research a national park and design a poster enticing people to visit it.

12 *Family Day* is the second Sunday in August. Have students decide on a family activity for that day and complete it.

13 *International Left-Handers Day* Assign some classwork to be written with the left hand only, or for left-handed students, with the right hand.

14 *Ernest Lawrence Thayer's* (who wrote *Casey at the Bat*) *Birthday* He was born in 1863. Read the poem *Casey at the Bat*. Then, have students write poems about their favorite sports.

15 *Middle Children's Day* Today is dedicated to children who are the middle child. Survey to see how many children are middle, youngest, oldest, and only. Graph the results.

16 **Klondike Gold Rush** began on this day in 1896. Paint rocks gold and let students weigh them.

17 **Davy Crockett's Birthday** Born in 1786, Davy Crockett told many tall tales about his hunting trips. Have students write tall tales.

18 **The Nineteenth Amendment** to the constitution, which gave **women the right to vote**, was **ratified** on this day in 1920. Provide students with things to vote on such as: choice of a story, math activity, etc. Let boys vote for something, then girls. Discuss how it feels not to have a vote.

19 **National Aviation Day** and **Orville Wright's Birthday** Let the children make paper airplanes. Practice flying the planes and measuring the distance each one travels.

20 **Water Quality Month** Discuss the importance of clean water with your class. Let them taste samples of bottled water, flavored water, and tap water. Did they taste a difference?

21 Hawaii became the **50th state** on this day in 1959. Have the children locate it on the map, do research, and make travel brochures.

22 **Be An Angel Day** Cut out angel wings to give to students when they're good. Have them write *I was an angel because....* Post the completed wings on the bulletin board.

23 **National Inventors Month** Ask each student to draw a picture of what they consider to be the greatest invention of all time and tell why they think it is the greatest.

24 Newspaper editor **Charles Dudley Warner** printed the statement, **"Everybody talks about the weather, but nobody does anything about it"** on this day in 1897. Have students write or tell what the weather would be like if they could control it.

25 **Be Kind to Humankind Week** is August 25-31. Brainstorm ways to show kindness to others. Ask students to take note when others exhibit kindness. Encourage students to share their classmates' good deeds with the class.

26 **Make Your Own Luck Day** The four-leaf clover is considered a symbol of good luck. Have students create their own good luck symbols and wear them for the day.

27 **Mother Teresa's Birthday** She was born in 1910. Make "just because " cards for a local convalescent home.

28 **Martin Luther King, Jr.** gave his **"I Have a Dream"** speech on this day in 1963. Cut out cloud shapes and have students write their dreams for a better world.

29 **Charlie "Bird" Parker's Birthday** He was an African-American jazz saxophonist. In 1920, many jazz musicians improvised in "jam sessions." Give students a variety of musical instruments and let them improvise.

30 **Mary Shelley's Birthday** Born in 1797, she wrote **Frankenstein**. Have students draw their own monsters and write a short story about them.

31 The **First U.S. Tennis Championships** were held on this day in 1881. Share a few rules of tennis with the class, such as how scores are kept (love, 15, 30, 40, deuce, game).

5

Sunday	Monday	Tuesday	Wednesday	Thursday	Friday	Saturday

AUGUST

© Carson-Dellosa CD-2090

AUGUST GAZETTE

Teacher _____ Date _____

IN THE NEWS

WHAT'S COMING UP

TAKE NOTE

KID'S CORNER

1. lhocos _____
2. sbu _____
3. naler _____
4. haect _____
5. scals _____

Celebrate August!

Dear Family Members,
Here are a few quick-and-easy activities to help you and your child celebrate special days throughout the month of August.

August is *Children's Good Manners Month*
- Remind your child to pay special attention to manners by remembering to treat others courteously. Have your child name ways he or she can be courteous at home and in school. Good manners include sharing, listening, helping, and taking turns.

August is *Sandwich Month*
- Have your child help you make fancy sandwiches by cutting slices of bread in different shapes using cookie cutters. Spread peanut butter, jam, or cream cheese on the shapes, or use the cookie cutter to cut your child's favorite lunch meat to make sandwiches.

Family Day is the second Sunday in August
- Help your child plan an outing where your family can do something enjoyable together. For example, have a picnic at a park, go swimming, or visit a children's museum! Indoor activities might include playing a board game or watching a special movie.

National Clown Week is August 1-7
- Set aside some time for "clowning around." You and your child can take turns acting silly and trying to make each other laugh. "Clowning around" can include telling jokes, making silly faces, or dressing up in clown costumes.

Smile Week is August 4-10
- Encourage smiles by creating and wearing smiley face badges. Help your child cut out large paper circles and decorate them like smiley faces. Pin or tape the badges to your shirts to wear during Smile Week. To make refrigerator magnets, add a piece of magnetic tape to a smiley face.

August 9 is *Smokey Bear's Birthday*
- In 1944, Smokey Bear became the symbol for the U.S. Forest Service to educate people on how to prevent forest fires. On this day in 1950, a cub that survived a forest fire was nursed back to health and became the living symbol of Smokey Bear. With your child, think of ways to prevent forest fires.

Hawaii became the 50th state on August 21, 1959
- Celebrate by making frozen pineapple treats. Drain two 20 oz. cans of crushed pineapple, reserving 2 tablespoons of juice. Pour pineapple, 2 tablespoons of lemon juice, 2 tablespoons of lime juice, $1/3$ cup of sugar, and reserved pineapple juice in a blender or food processor. Blend until smooth. Pour the mixture into one-quart resealable freezer bags. Place the bags flat in a freezer for $1^1/2$ hours or until slushy. Then, pour the mixture into drinking glasses. Makes 8 servings.

Read In August!

Dear Family Members,
Here are some books to share with your child to enhance the enjoyment of reading in August.

 Helping Out by George Ancona
- *Photographs show kids working with adults in various settings.*
- Ask your child to choose his or her favorite task from the story, then allow him or her to help you with it.

 The Little Engine that Could by Watty Piper
- *This timeless tale of perseverance tells of a little engine that is determined to get over a mountain.*
- Share with your child an experience you had where you had to try very hard to do something. Encourage your child to share a similar experience with you.

 Norma Jean, Jumping Bean by Joanna Cole
- *Norma Jean loves to jump, but she learns a lesson about self-discipline when she realizes that there is a time and a place for jumping.*
- Ask your child to tell what he or she would do as the main character in the story. How would he or she solve the problem?

 A Sip of Aesop by Jane Yolen
- *Colorful illustrations and poetic meter put a twist on Aesop's traditional fables.*
- Have your child pick his or her favorite fable and retell it in his or her own words.

 Into the Sea by Brenda Z. Guiberson
- *Follows the life of a sea turtle from its hatching to its return to the island to lay eggs.*
- Provide a paper plate, colored paper, scissors, glue, and crayons. Have your child make a paper plate turtle using the craft supplies.

 Going on a Whale Watch by Bruce McMillan
- *Two children go on a whale-watching boat and see several kinds of whales doing such things as diving and breaching.*
- Pretend you and your child are on a whale-watching boat. Take turns describing what you see and hear.

 Monarch Butterfly by Gail Gibbons
- *Beautiful, bright pictures describe the life cycle and migration of the monarch butterfly.*
- Have your child draw a picture of a colorful butterfly. Cut out the butterfly and tie it to the end of a straw so children can "flutter" them around the room.

September

Day-by-Day Calendar

1 *Library Card Sign Up Month* Plan a class field trip to the public library. Before the trip, request library card applications for the children to fill out.

Jonesburg Public Library
Library Card
Name_____ Date_____
Address_____

2 *Birthday of the U.S. Treasury* Provide students with circles or rectangular paper to design an original bill or coin of their choice.

3 *Aliki's Birthday* This children's author and illustrator was born in 1920. Read a book written by Aliki. Have students draw a picture to illustrate something that happened in the story.

4 *National Ethnic Foods Month* Have your class pick a country. Then, celebrate that country by having a party and enjoying its native foods.

5 *Substitute Teacher Appreciation Week* is September 5-11. Have the class make cards for substitute teachers. When the class has a substitute teacher for a day, send one to the substitute.

Thank You

6 *National School Success Month* Make a "School's Cool" bulletin board. Cut apple shapes from construction paper. Have students write two reasons why they like school on the apples. Post on a bulletin board.

7 *Anna Mary "Grandma" Moses' Birthday* This American primitive painter was born in 1860. Find pictures of her paintings and share them with the children.

8 *Do It! Day (Fight Procrastination Day)* Have the class participate in a "spring" cleaning or any other job that has been put off for too long.

9 *National Literacy Month* Brainstorm a list of favorite books with students. Put some of the books in a learning center. Allow students to read these books during free time, or read one to the class as a reward for good behavior.

10 *Save the Tiger Month* Have students "save" any tigers they find in magazines, newspapers, ads, storybooks, etc. Ask students to bring them in to post on a bulletin board.

11 *Public Lands Day* Plan to pick up trash at a local park with the class.

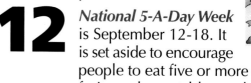

12 *National 5-A-Day Week* is September 12-18. It is set aside to encourage people to eat five or more servings of fruits and vegetables each day. Have students bring in different fruits and vegetables to sample.

13 *Roald Dahl's Birthday* The author of *Charlie and the Chocolate Factory* was born in 1916. Watch *Willie Wonka and the Chocolate Factory* to celebrate.

14 *International Cross-Cultural Day* Study a different country with the class today. Learn how to say a few words in the country's native language.

15 *Tomie DePaola's Birthday* This children's author, born in 1934, wrote and illustrated *Strega Nona*, *Pancakes for Breakfast*, and other books. Read one of his books to the class.

10

16 *The Mayflower left England* for the New World today in 1620. Have students make their own Mayflowers out of milk cartons. Cut the tops off milk cartons and staple straws to the sides. Decorate the boats and make sails to attach to the straws.

17 *National Piano Month* Bring in some music featuring this instrument to share with the class.

18 *National Student Day* Put each student's name in a hat. Have each student choose a name (if they pick their own, have them draw again). Then, ask each student to write something good about the student they chose to share with the class.

19  International "I Love You" sign *Deaf Awareness Week* is the last week of September. Teach students short phrases or the alphabet in sign language.

20 *National Kids' Day* Allow students to share with the class something they love doing (singing, reading, writing, playing sports, etc.). If possible, have them perform for the class.

21 *National Chicken Month* Have students bring in chicken recipes from home. Make a copy of each recipe for each child in the class. Then, have students make "Kickin' Chicken" Recipe Books to share with their families.

22 *Italo Marchiony invented the first ice-cream cone* today in 1903. Have students draw a picture of their favorite flavors and toppings.

23 *First Day of Autumn* Have students do crayon rubbings of leaves. Compare and contrast the shapes, vein patterns, etc.

24 *Native American Day* is the fourth Friday in September. Some Native Americans used totem poles to record superstition, life, and legends. Have students create totem poles using long cardboard tubes.

25 The *first newspaper* in America *was published* in 1690. Have students create a class newspaper.

26 *Good Neighbor Day* A neighbor isn't just someone who lives next door. Brainstorm definitions of neighbors. Then, have a class discussion on ways to be a good neighbor.

27 *World Gratitude Day, Inc. was established* in 1965. Have students make a list of all the things for which they are grateful. Then, have them illustrate one.

28 *Confucius' Birthday* He was born in 551 B.C. Have students write advice on paper strips and glue them to brown triangle "fortune cookies," then display on a bulletin board.

29 The first *telephone answering machine was introduced* today in 1950. Bring in a tape recorder or answering machine and have students write and record creative messages.

30 *National Honey Month* Sample different kinds of honey (clover, orange blossom, and sage).

11

September

Sunday	Monday	Tuesday	Wednesday	Thursday	Friday	Saturday

September Gazette

Teacher _____ Date _____

IN THE NEWS

TAKE NOTE

WHAT'S COMING UP

KID'S CORNER

Celebrate September!

Dear Family Members,
Here are a few quick-and-easy activities to help you and your child celebrate special days throughout the month of September.

September is *National Honey Month*
- Serve vanilla ice cream and let your child pour honey over the scoop for a delicious treat! You can also eat honey on pancakes or waffles, on toast, or use it as a sweetener in tea.

September is *National Literacy Month*
- Set aside time for family members to read silently or take turns reading stories aloud. Encourage each person to describe a favorite story and explain why they like it, then draw a favorite scene from the story.

Labor Day **is celebrated on the first Monday in September**
- Have family members tell about the jobs and chores they do daily or weekly. Jobs can include washing clothes, making the bed, cooking dinner, etc. Have everyone pitch in and help with household chores or yard work, then enjoy some well-deserved time off.

Grandparents Day **is celebrated on the first Sunday in September following Labor Day**
- Celebrate this special day by helping your child make picture frames to give as gifts. Find photographs or have the child draw pictures of himself or herself with his or her grandparents. Cut out frame shapes from poster board and have the child decorate them. Glue the frames over the pictures, then glue another piece of poster board behind them. Attach magnetic tape to the backs so the pictures can be displayed on a refrigerator.

Italo Marchiony invented the first ice cream cone **on September 22, 1903**
- Enjoy ice cream treats in honor of this occasion. Make ice cream cups by pressing a warm, waffle into the bottom of a small bowl. Allow the waffle to cool to room temperature in the bowl. Then, allow your child to fill the waffle with a favorite flavor of ice cream and top with candy sprinkles.

September 23 is the *First Day of Autumn*
- Hunt for colorful autumn leaves outside with your child. Help your child make a leaf collage by gluing the leaves to construction paper. If desired, use a Tree Identification Guide to label each leaf with its name.

September 26 is *Johnny Appleseed's Birthday*
- John Chapman, also known as Johnny Appleseed, was born on this day in 1774. Johnny is thought to have planted numerous apple orchards throughout the United States. Slice several different kinds of apples, dip them in peanut butter or honey, and enjoy them as a snack with your child.

Read In September!

Dear Family Members,
Here are some books to share with your child to enhance the enjoyment of reading in September.

Abuela by Arthur Dorros
- *While riding a bus with her grandmother, a little girl imagines that they are flying over New York City, visiting people and sites from her grandmother's past.*
- Have your child ask a grandparent to tell about places and people that were important to him or her.

I Don't Want to Go Back to School by Marisabina Russo
- *A little boy is worried and anxious about starting second grade.*
- Share a story about a time when you were afraid. Encourage you child to share a similar experience with you.

This Is the Way We Go to School by Edith Baer
- *Lovely watercolor illustrations depict how children in different parts of the United States and around the world travel to school.*
- Have your child draw a picture showing how he or she travels to school.

Miss Malarkey Doesn't Live in Room 10 by Judy Finchler
- *When his teacher moves into the same apartment building, a first grade boy realizes she does not live at school.*
- Have your child tell his or her favorite part of the story and explain why.

Johnny Appleseed by Steven Kellogg
- *Tells the story of this legendary man and his travels throughout America.*
- Ask your child to tell about what food he or she would want to share with other people and explain why.

Apple Pie Tree by Zoe Hall
- *Two sisters watch their apple tree throughout the seasons, waiting for the fruit to be picked and used for pies in autumn.*
- Have your child draw a picture of what an apple pie tree would look like.

Grandfather's Journey by Allen Say
- *Using beautiful paintings, the author illustrates the story of his grandfather's travels between America and Japan.*
- Work with your child to write a letter to a grandparent asking about a trip he or she took.

Student of the Week!

_____
Name

_____
Signed

_____
Date

© Carson-Dellosa CD-2090

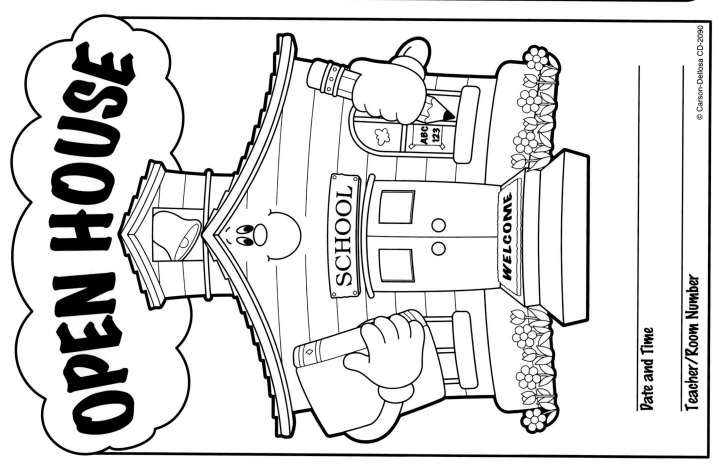

OPEN HOUSE

SCHOOL

WELCOME

ABC 123

© Carson-Dellosa CD-2090

_____
Date and Time

_____
Teacher/Room Number

16

WELCOME TO SCHOOL!

NAME

TEACHER'S SIGNATURE

© Carson-Dellosa CD-2090

© Carson-Dellosa CD-2090

"A-peel-ing" Work

Name

Date

17

AUGUST
Writing Activities

As summer blazes to an end and excited faces fill your classroom, engage students in writing! Focus on topics that will cause children to appreciate unique events this month, get to know each other better, and to settle into their new routines. Happy new school year!

Heat Beaters

HOT!

Warm

Cool

Cold

August is a good time to help students compile a *Top Ten Ways to Beat the Heat* list. Have each student come up with five usual (eat ice cream) or unusual (sit on ice cream) ways to cool off. Post all the ideas on a bulletin board and have students come by and vote for their favorites by putting check marks and their initials by two of them. Tally the votes to create a *Top Ten* list and publish it in your August newsletter. Reward the class for their contributions with a cool treat such as ice cream!

You've Got a Friend

The beginning of a new school year is an ideal time to make new friends. Discuss the value of friendship with the class and ask students to write about a time when they either needed a friend or were a friend. Call on volunteers to share their special stories.

Yummy Watermelon

National Watermelon Day is August 3. Students may be interested to know that watermelons are 92% water, and the world record for the largest watermelon is 225 pounds. Serve watermelon as a special snack and then supply students with red, green, and black construction paper to make watermelon slices. Ask students to write similes (comparisons using *like* or *as*) about watermelon on the slices. For example, *watermelons taste like sunshine, are as red as roses, as juicy as..., as sweet as...,* etc. Post the crafts and the facts about watermelon on a bulletin board titled *Watermelon—What a Melon!*

Watermelons taste like sunshine

Good Advice

Students can show off their problem solving skills with this activity. Have students come up with their own back-to-school advice by pretending to be newspaper columnists. Write the following letter on the board and have each child compose a response. Place the responses in a center and allow students to enjoy reading the advice.

DEAR COLUMNIST,
I'M HAVING TROUBLE GETTING UP EVERY MORNING AND GETTING USED TO SCHOOL AFTER A LONG SUMMER VACATION.
CAN YOU HELP ME?
SIGNED,
SLEEPY SUE

Dear Sleepy Sue,
Getting up after a good summer is hard. Try going to bed on time at night. You could use an alarm clock or get your parents to help also.
Signed,
Doug

I like good grades in spelling and winning a race, but friends especially bring a smile to my face!

Smile When You Say That! ☺

The first week of August is National Smile Week. Ask students to list three-five things about being back in school that make them smile and to then create a poem from that list. Have each child write her finished poem in the shape of a smile.

Editor's Checklist

Create an editor's checklist for students to use when turning in work. Include items such as:

☑ *Name and date are on my paper.*

☑ *I have checked my spelling.*

☑ *All sentences have the correct punctuation mark at the end.*

☑ *Every sentence begins with a capital letter.*

☑ *I read the sentences, and they make sense.*

Have students use the checklist and make any corrections before turning in their work.

What's Under the Beach Umbrella?

Take a trip to the shore! Have students staple and decorate a piece of colorful paper to resemble a beach umbrella. Staple this page over a sheet of writing paper. Have students write about what is under the beach umbrella when the umbrella is lifted.

I am a seaweed covered sea monster that crawled out of the ocean to catch some rays.

What's under the Beach Umbrella?

SEPTEMBER Writing Activities

Computer Spelling

Students can learn by listening with this activity. Tape record yourself reading and spelling each week's spelling words. Put the tape, along with a tape player, next to a class computer. Have students practice their spelling words by listening to the tape, then typing the words. Students can print their lists and check them against a written spelling list.

Summer turns to fall during September! The most obvious change is that children everywhere are back in school! Use these fun September writing activities that focus on creative expression to ease students into a new school year.

Word Bank Words

friend	smile	welcome
apple	chalkboard	playground
school	crayon	teacher
bushel	pencil	paper
cider	notebook	school

All About Me

Build self-esteem by having students write tributes to themselves in which they name good things about themselves and why people like them.

Getting to Know You

Help students get to know each other by interviewing a partner about things they like. The list may include things students like to eat, wear, watch, do, etc. Then, have students write paragraphs describing these things. Encourage students to share their work with others as a way to get to know each other.

The Sounds of September

Students will create sound sensations with these creative poems. Explain to students that some words, such as *bang* and *zip*, make the sounds of what they mean. These words are called *onomatopoeia*. Have students generate a list of onomatopoeic (ah nuh mah tuh PE ik) words for September, then write onomatopoeic poems with the words.

September

RING, RING goes the school bell.

Rumble, rumble goes the bus.

Chitter-chatter go the students.

WHEE...yell all of us.

by Anita

Letters to New Students

Start the new school year with memories from the previous year. Students can write letters to students starting school in their previous grade. In the letters, students can explain things they can look forward to during the year and important things for them to remember as they start the new year.

Johnny Smith
Grade 3
Mr. Jones

Grade 2 Students
Ms. Plummer's Class

INK

Two-Word Poems

Keep it short and sweet! Ask students to think about what they like most about being back in school, then write two-word poems on the subject. Tell students to make their two-word poems as short or as long as they wish, but each line should contain only two words.

Back-to-School

Up early
Bus ride
Friends everywhere
Paper, pencil
Story time!

My Ultimate Playground

A 500-foot slide? Swings that can swing into outerspace? Have students write directions for how to design the ultimate playground. What would they include on the playground? What materials would things be made of? Then, have each student illustrate his imaginary ultimate playground to display with his writing.

Editing Partners

Double up and get it right! Assign each student a partner and have them proofread each other's papers for spelling, capitalization, and punctuation. Allow different partners to work together throughout the year.

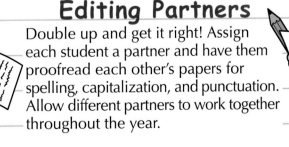

Bulletin Board Ideas

Let the learning begin with this welcoming bulletin board. Cover a bulletin board with blue paper. Enlarge the bus pattern (page 42) onto yellow construction paper. Give each child a large piece of construction paper and have him draw and label a self-portrait. Children can then cut out the self-portraits and place them in the bus windows. Make sure you also include a self-portrait of you as the bus driver. This display works well with the *Let the Learning Begin* unit (pages 28-42).

Spotlight upcoming events and topics. Cover a bulletin board with black paper. Cut out and attach several white circles around the edges of the board to resemble a movie marquee. Put crafts, book covers, and upcoming topics on the board. This display can accompany the *Let the Learning Begin* unit (pages 28-42).

This tasty display will encourage good behavior. Cover a bulletin board with aluminum foil to resemble a cookie sheet. Make paper chocolate chip cookies, attach resealable plastic bags labeled with student names to the bottom of the board, and put five cookies in each bag. Place sentence strips with children's names on the board. When a student exhibits good behavior, attach a cookie from her bag near her name. When she has five cookies on the board, reward her—with a real cookie, of course! This display goes well with the *Building Good Character* chapter (pages 43-56).

Your class will have good manners covered with a good manners quilt! Provide 5" x 5" squares of light-colored construction paper. Have each child write his name and illustrate a phrase about good manners on a square. Alternate blue and yellow squares for a checkerboard effect, and add a colorful border with stitching. The good manners quilt works well with the manners section of the *Building Good Character* chapter (pages 43-56).

Let your students teach each other to "bee" their best by helping you create this honey of a bulletin board. Cover the board with yellow paper. Display an enlarged beehive pattern (page 54) in the center of the board. Give each student a bee pattern (page 54). Have him color it, write his name on the wing, then write about and illustrate a time when he was at his best. Display completed papers around the beehive with bee accents. You may wish to use this bulletin board with the *Building Good Character* chapter (pg. 43-56).

Get to know students and their friends with this picture perfect display. Cover a bulletin board with bright green paper. Have students bring in photographs of themselves with friends, or photograph students in the classroom. Students can use art supplies to create cute frames to tape over the pictures, attach the photos to the board, then share their pictures with the class. Be sure to include your own pictures for the activity, as well! This display can accompany the Friendship section of the *Building Good Character* chapter (pg. 43-56).

24

Students will blossom with delight when completing this display. Cover a bulletin board with light blue paper. In the center, draw a large tree with several branches. Paint the tree using brown tempera paint. Have students cut out apple blossom patterns (page 62) and glue crumpled pieces of pink tissue paper to the blossoms. Hang outstanding student papers from the branches, highlighting them with the apple blossoms. This bulletin board goes well with the *A Bushel of Apple Fun* chapter (pg. 57-62).

Show students that good work is the apple of your eye! Cover the top ⅔ of a bulletin board with sky blue paper and the bottom ⅓ with green paper. Add white cotton batting clouds to the sky. Copy three apple patterns (page 62) for each student to color. Let each student cut out a paper basket, write her name on it, and glue a photograph or self-portrait on one apple, then write a fact about herself on the remaining two apples. Place each child's apples in her basket. Title the display *An A-peel-ing Bunch*, and use it to accompany the *A Bushel of Apple Fun* chapter (pg. 57-62).

Give children a view of the big picture about community life! Assign children to four groups, and give each group a piece of paper that will cover about ¼ of the bulletin board. Let groups create a picture of our planet, country, state, and city or town. Each group should create one picture to become part of the "big picture." Post the largest community first (the world), then the country, state, etc. You can pair this board with the *Community Counts* chapter (pg. 63-75).

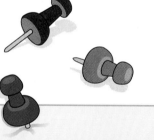

Children will line up at this display to guess what kinds of helpers their classmates want to be. Have pairs of children trace each other's outlines on butcher paper and cut them out, then decorate to look like community helpers. Finally, let the pairs think of clues describing their helpers to post with the outlines in cut-out speech balloons. Change the outlines on the bulletin board until all have been posted. This display may be used with the Community Helpers section in the *Community Counts* unit (pg. 63-75).

Let this sparkling display help grandparents feel appreciated when visiting your class. Cover the display area with blue paper. Have each child illustrate and label a special grandparent memory on a sheet of paper. Then, use plastic jewels or sequins to frame the pictures. Post the pretty framed pictures on the bulletin board during *The Grandest Celebration* chapter (pg. 78-80).

Divide a bulletin board into three sections. Label them *By Air They Fly*, *By Water They Swim*, and *By Land They Walk and Run*. Write the names of migrating animals on sentence strips. Ask students to post the strips with the correct heading, and then draw or cut pictures from magazines to add to the display. Older students can include index cards beside each animal telling why and where it migrates. This display can be the focus of the *Animals on the Move* chapter (pg. 81-92).

LET THE LEARNING BEGIN!

Summer is over and now it's time for the *real* fun–and the learning–to begin! These ideas for the beginning of the school year will help you welcome your students back to school in style, teach students ever-important rules and regulations, and have a memorable, meaningful open house. On your mark...get set...and go forward into a successful school year!

Did You Know?

🍎 The first school was established by Egyptians in 3000 B.C.

🍎 Colonists in Massachusetts created public schools that were open to all children in 1647.

🍎 Currently, children in Japan average about 220 school days per year, while students in the United States and France average about 180 school days per year.

Literature Selections

I Don't Want to Go Back to School
by Marisabina Russo
Greenwillow, 1994
(Picture book, 32 pg.)
A student is panicked about returning to school, but learns that it isn't so bad after all.

School Days
by B. G. Hennessy
Puffin, 1992.
(Picture book, 32 pg.)
Rhyming text captures interesting events at the beginning of the school year.

Miss Malarkey Doesn't Live in Room 10
by Kevin O'Malley
Walker and Co., 1996
(Picture book, 32 pg.)
A student discovers that teachers have lives outside of school.

Never Spit on Your Shoes
by Denys Cazet
Orchard Books, 1993
(Picture book, 32 pg.)
Arnie, a puppy, comes home from his first day of school.

Welcome to School!

Put a new spin on show-and-tell with this getting-to-know-you activity. Mail (or hand out at a before-school orientation) a letter to each student that welcomes him to your class, along with a personalized name tag for the student to wear on the first day of school. Greet students by name when they enter the classroom. On the first day of school, give each student a paper lunch bag and tell him to place inside the bag a "mystery" object from home that tells something about him, and bring the bag to school the next day. Then, call on each student to come to the front of the class, introduce himself, and play *10 Questions* by inviting the class to ask yes/no questions about the object in the bag. Once the object has been guessed, have the student show the object and explain how it relates to him.

28

There's No Place Like School!

Make the first day less hectic for you and your students by providing some fun work. Place a blank desk name tag or cubbie marker on each student's desk. When students arrive, play relaxing music and provide crayons and markers for students to personalize their name tags and draw pictures on their cubbie markers of things they want to learn during the upcoming school year. By keeping students busy and happy, you will be available to complete all those first-day teacher tasks!

What's in a Name?

Students can find out if the name fits the classmate! Locate a baby name book with meanings of names. Give each student an index card with her name on it. Read aloud the meaning of each student's name and have her write it under her name on the card. Use art materials to decorate the name cards. On the backs of the cards, allow older students to write whether they think the meanings of their names are accurate for them and why.

Tell-All

Play this game to "break the ice" on the first day of school. Sit in a circle. Pass pencils and a pad of self-stick notes around the circle. Ask each child to take a pencil and one to five self-stick notes. Each child should write one fact about herself on each note pad page. Go around the circle and share all of the facts. Then, write the names on a bulletin board and display the notes beside each name.

Go to the Head of the Class

Get students moving to find things they have in common. Write characteristics on 3" x 5" index cards, such as *I have a pet, I went to the beach this summer, I am the youngest in my family, I like reading, Pizza is my favorite food, I play soccer*, etc. Place the cards in a bag, pull out one at a time, and read the characteristic to the class. Invite all students who match the characteristic to come to the front of the class and say their names one at a time. After each characteristic has been read, challenge each student to recall the name of a classmate with whom he shares an attribute.

   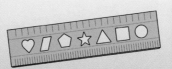

29

Bingo Was His Name-O

Play a fun game of "Name-O" using students' names. List names on the board and distribute copies of the Name-O card pattern (page 40). Tell students to randomly write their classmates' names in the boxes on their Name-O cards. Place student names written on small sheets of paper in a bag. Draw a name from the bag, call it out, and have that student stand up briefly. Use dried beans or other manipulatives to place on a name when it is called out. The first child to cover a row horizontally, diagonally, or vertically is the winner. When someone calls *Name-O!*, read out the names on the winning row and then identify the matching students.

Whoooooo's Missing ??????

After students know each others' names, have them play a missing student name game. Have students place their heads on their desks and close their eyes. Quietly walk around the classroom, tap a student on the shoulder, and have her go outside the classroom. Once she is out of sight, have the remaining students look around and see if they can identify who is missing.

One-on-One Interview <u>Fun!</u>

Encourage creativity with unusual interviews. Brainstorm a list of silly questions, such as, *If you could be a food, what would you be? Which animal do you think is the scariest? What is your favorite planet, and why? If you could change your name, what would you change it to?* Write the list on the board. Have students interview partners and record each other's answers. Then, sit together in a circle. Ask each pair to introduce each other and tell all of the silly answers they learned.

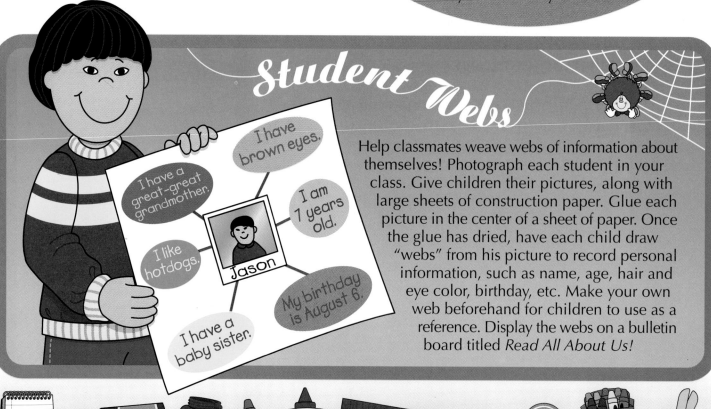

Student Webs

Help classmates weave webs of information about themselves! Photograph each student in your class. Give children their pictures, along with large sheets of construction paper. Glue each picture in the center of a sheet of paper. Once the glue has dried, have each child draw "webs" from his picture to record personal information, such as name, age, hair and eye color, birthday, etc. Make your own web beforehand for children to use as a reference. Display the webs on a bulletin board titled *Read All About Us!*

"All About Me" Boxes

Use cereal boxes to turn *All About Me* information into a three-dimensional display. Provide an empty cereal box for each student. Have students cover the cereal boxes with tempera paint, then draw and label pictures on construction paper shapes to glue to the sides of the boxes. Pictures might be titled *Me, My Family, My Favorite Food, My Birthday, My Favorite Book, What I Like Most about School, My Favorite Subject, When I Grow up, I Want to Be…*, etc. Display the boxes on a class bookshelf and allow students time to look at the display and learn about their classmates.

Reading around School

Students will get to know their school and some new words, too! Before school begins, walk around and take pictures of signs, including *Exit, Fire Extinguisher, Restroom*, etc. Display the pictures on a wall or bulletin board and call on students to read or describe the signs and discuss the meanings of the words and symbols. After all signs have been identified, take a walk around the school and find the signs that match the photographs.

Tasty Teamwork!

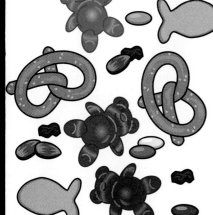

Working together means eating together with this delicious, kid-friendly community recipe. Have ingredients and measuring tools available to mix up this snack. If possible, divide the class into groups of four and have each student in a group measure out ¹/₄ cup of each ingredient so everyone will have the opportunity to mix ingredients for the snack.

Ingredients

- 1 cup of **teamwork** *(fish-shaped crackers)*
- 1 cup of **cooperation** *(sunflower seeds)*
- 1 cup of **respect** *(raisins)*
- 1 cup of **caring** *(candy-coated chocolate)*
- 1 cup of **fairness** *(pretzels)*
- 1 cup of **doing our best** *(fruit-flavored, bear-shaped gummy candy)*

31

My Area of Expertise

Make children comfortable in a new classroom by letting them demonstrate or tell about something they can do well. Ask each child to think of something he can do well, such as ride a bike with two wheels, read, care for a pet, etc. Let each child draw himself performing his activity, and give a silly "superhero" title to the picture, such as *Sam the Super Speller* or *Rebeccah Queen Kitty Feeder*. Post the areas-of-expertise pictures around the room so that children can look at their artwork for an instant boost of confidence!

Name Sorting

Reinforce phonetic sounds and patterns while learning each others' names. Have each student write his first name on a section of sentence strip or an index card. Show a student's card for reference, then have the class name the beginning sound, ending sound, vowel combinations, or other sound in the student's name. Then, choose attributes of the name to sort with other students' names. For example, if the name is *Michael,* invite other students whose names begin with *M* to come forward and show their cards. Other options would be to call students whose names have two syllables, whose names end in *l*, whose names contain the *ae* digraph, etc. Continue the activity using all the names.

Put a new twist on the usual *What I did this summer* activity with this fun, interactive memory game, and be sure to have an atlas handy! Sit in a circle in alphabetical order by the first letter of children's first names. Each child will tell her name and then make up a place she went over the summer that begins with the first letter of her name. It can be a street in the community, a city, a state, a country, even a planet. She must also remember what each child said before her! For example, the first child may say *My name is Amber and I went to Australia this summer.* The next child may say *This is Amber and she went to Australia. My name is Brad and I went to Burlington this summer,* and so on. For younger children, eliminate the memory part of the game and simply let them take turns thinking of places which begin with the first letter of each child's name.

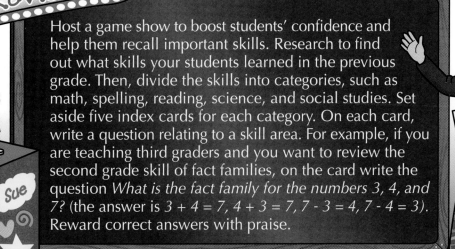

Game Show Review

Host a game show to boost students' confidence and help them recall important skills. Research to find out what skills your students learned in the previous grade. Then, divide the skills into categories, such as math, spelling, reading, science, and social studies. Set aside five index cards for each category. On each card, write a question relating to a skill area. For example, if you are teaching third graders and you want to review the second grade skill of fact families, on the card write the question *What is the fact family for the numbers 3, 4, and 7?* (the answer is *3 + 4 = 7, 4 + 3 = 7, 7 - 3 = 4, 7 - 4 = 3*). Reward correct answers with praise.

Numbers and Me

Challenge students to find out how important numbers are in everyday life. Ask students to recall some number skills that they learned in previous grades. Help them recall times when they have used numbers, such as counting the number of students in class, remembering the school bus number, cooking (measurement), or figuring out their allowances (money, addition, etc.) Distribute large sheets of light-colored construction paper and markers or crayons. Have each student write his name at the top of the paper, then draw a large "tic-tac-toe" design on the paper and illustrate a self-portrait in the middle square. In the remaining eight squares, draw objects with other important numbers, such as his bus number, classroom number, birthday written numerically, age, phone number, channel number and time of his favorite TV show, etc.

? Guess What I Did Today!

Start a family discussion about students' exciting first day or week of school with a take-home letter. Copy and distribute a Back-to-School Letter (page 38). Have each student fill in the blanks on the letter. You may wish to let children share answers with each other. Have students take the letters home to share with their families.

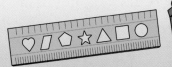

33

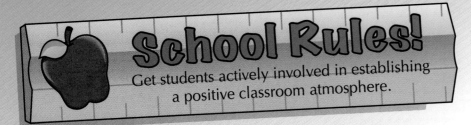

School Rules!

Get students actively involved in establishing a positive classroom atmosphere.

Who Makes the Rules?

Involving students in decisions about classroom rules makes the rules more important and meaningful to the students. Brainstorm a list of rules to make the class safe and fun. Also generate a list of consequences for not following the rules that the class agrees are fair. Display the rules and consequences on a wall beside an enlarged ice cream cone pattern (page 41). Each day the class follows the classroom rules, write the date on an ice cream pattern (page 41) and place it on top of the cone. When students receive a predetermined number of ice cream scoops, reward the class with an ice cream party! You can also complete this exercise with fire-drill rules, lunchroom rules, etc.

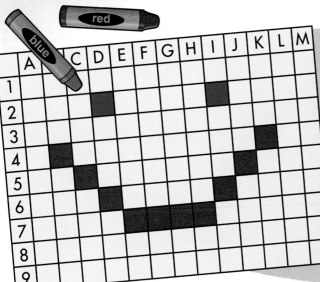

You Make Me Smile!

Let students complete this grid picture to discover how you feel when they follow directions. Each student needs a blank, numbered grid (page 40) and two crayons. Use the sample to give directions on how to fill in the squares, such as, *Use your blue crayon to fill in square D, 2. Use your red crayon to fill in square K, 4.* Instruct students to listen carefully because you will not repeat any instructions. When all the directions are given, ask the class to hold up their pictures, and see which good listeners make the teacher smile!

Kindness Counts!

Teach students that an important part of school is learning how to treat others politely. Brainstorm a list of polite words and phrases, such as *please, may I, thank you,* etc. Divide children into small groups and give each group a section of bulletin board paper. Have them draw themselves in a school situation using speech bubbles with polite phrases. Place the drawings side by side on a wall to create a mural to display as a reminder of how children should treat each other throughout the year.

Bus Safety "Rule Play"

Make bus safety a must for students. Brainstorm bus safety rules, or use the list provided. Assign a bus rule to each pair of students, then have them write the rule on an enlarged bus pattern (page 42), and decorate it by gluing small magazine pictures of children in the bus windows. Then, let each pair make up and perform a skit demonstrating the rule. Post the buses on a wall or bulletin board with the title *Climb on Board with Bus Safety*.

School Bus Rules

- Be at the bus stop a little early.
- Leave pets at home.
- Stay off the street at the bus stop.
- Dress appropriately for the weather.
- Get on and off the bus in a single-file line.
- No pushing or running.
- Stand back from the bus until it has completely stopped.
- Cross far in front of the bus and only when lights are flashing.
- Look both ways before crossing the street.
- Sit down quickly, face front, and stay seated throughout the ride.
- Talk quietly.
- Keep arms, legs, and belongings out of the aisle and inside the bus.
- In case of an emergency, stay quiet and calm. Listen for directions from the driver.
- Keep hands, feet, and objects to yourself.

Hooray for the Bus Driver!

Make a special treat to thank bus drivers for giving safe rides to school every day. Talk about what an important job being a bus driver is. Then, divide students into groups according to how many buses pick up children at your school (include walkers and car riders in each group). Give each group a plastic jar or can with a resealable lid (peanut butter jars work well), four milk or juice jug lids, and yellow and black paint. Let students paint the containers yellow and the lids black. When the paint is dry, place the containers on their sides to glue the milk or juice lids near the bottom of the containers to represent wheels. Add bus details such as windows and lights. Fill the containers with snack mix (you may want to use the recipe from *Tasty Teamwork!* page 31). Close each lid and attach a thank-you card signed by the group members. Designate students to present the gifts to the bus drivers.

All around the Playground

Before letting children play, make sure they have safety on the brain. Let students demonstrate the proper way to use each piece of equipment, including balls, bats, jump ropes, etc. When recess is over, create safety posters for the equipment, including directions on how to use the equipment properly and illustrations showing correct use and incorrect use. Display the posters in the classroom.

35

Open House

Let your class help you get ready for an Open House, then make sure parents and students enjoy the time they spend there!

A Personal Invitation

Personalized invitations are a great way to spread the word about an upcoming open house. Fill in Open House information on a copy of the schoolhouse pattern (page 42), and reproduce it for each student to color. Fold a piece of construction paper in half. On the back of the schoolhouse, tape an accordion-folded strip of construction paper, then attach the strip to the inside of the card. The schoolhouse will "pop up" when the card is opened. Decorate the fronts of the cards with parents' names and then send the cards home. Continue the schoolhouse theme by letting students write their names on additional patterns and using them as desk name plates.

This Is My Classroom

Involve students in the presentation of Open House topics. Reserve a video camera and assign small groups to make short video clips of different areas of the classroom or of procedures that you would like to introduce and explain to parents. For example, have a group explain what happens during center time, and then demonstrate a few center activities. Play the video on Open House night to help parents understand your classroom community and see firsthand how their children are involved in activities.

Get-to-Know-Me Questionnaire

To provide parents and students with an opportunity to share important information, and to help keep them occupied while you meet and greet new arrivals, place Parent/Student Open House Questionnaires (page 39) on every desk for students and parents to complete at Open House. This information will assist you in meeting individual students' needs, and it will also let parents know that you appreciate their input and recommendations for a successful school year!

My Special Folder

Store important papers in important folders! If you have papers or student work to show parents at Open House, have students decorate file folders with copies of the schoolhouse and school bus patterns (page 42). This will make the process of reviewing paperwork a pleasure indeed! After the Open House, use the decorated folders to store student papers, or to send important notes home to parents.

Mom and Dad, Find My Desk!

Students will get a kick out of watching their parents use their thinking skills in the classroom! Have students write a few descriptive sentences about themselves on sentence strips, such as *I am a boy with curly black hair and brown eyes. Baseball is my favorite sport.* Remove any name tags from desks and replace them with the sentences. Challenge parents to locate their child's desk by reading the sentences and guessing if the description fits their child.

These Are My Parents

It's a treat for children to have their parents at school, so take advantage of it. Before beginning your orientation, go around the room and have each child tell his parents' names. To expand the activity, ask children to tell their parents' occupations as well.

Make It Fun for the Kids!

If you need an opportunity to discuss classroom policies and procedures with parents, keep the children occupied during this time with an activity table set up on one side of your classroom. Include books, art materials, and manipulatives that children can quietly use while their parents listen to important Open House information.

Open House Trivia

Play a game of Open House Trivia with parents to provide a fun, relaxed atmosphere. Brainstorm questions students can ask their parents during Open House, such as *What is the school principal's name? What did your child eat for lunch today? What does the 'caboose' helper do?*, etc. Take turns asking questions. Have small tokens available and give a token to each parent who is the first to raise his hand and then answer a question correctly. Award a small prize, such as a school T-shirt or stuffed animal of the school's mascot, to the parent who wins the most tokens.

37

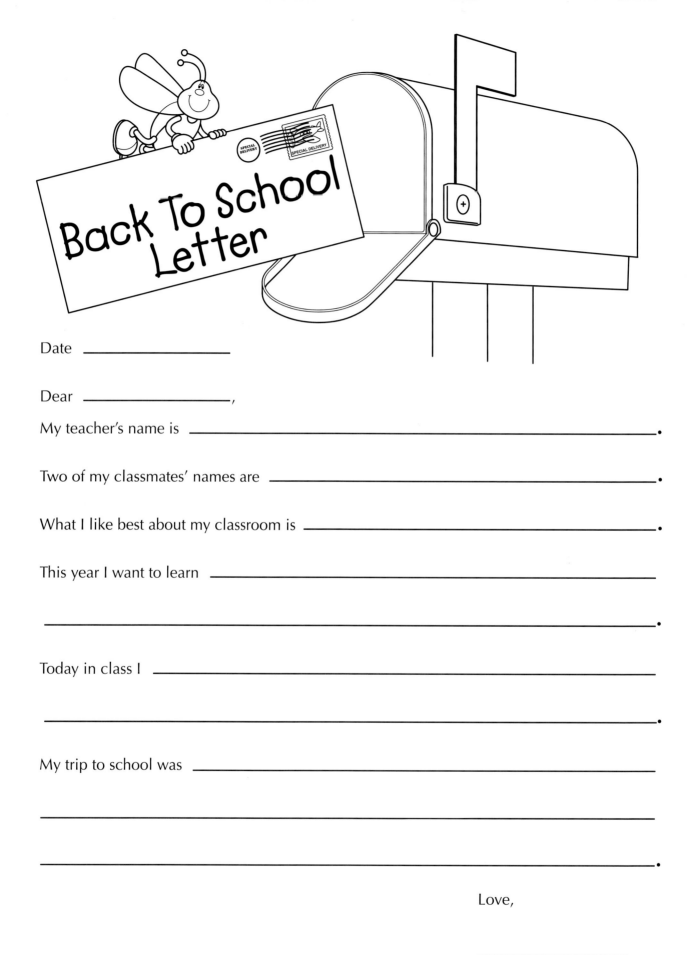

Back To School Letter

Date _____

Dear _____,

My teacher's name is _____.

Two of my classmates' names are _____.

What I like best about my classroom is _____.

This year I want to learn _____

_____.

Today in class I _____

_____.

My trip to school was _____

_____

_____.

Love,

_____

Parent/Student Open House Questionnaire

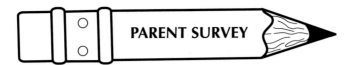

Parent name _____   Date _____

Student Name _____

1. What types of activities does your child enjoy? _____

2. How would you describe your child's attitude toward school? _____

3. What skills and subject areas are the strongest for your child? _____

4. What skills and subject areas does your child need to work on? _____

5. Does your child enjoy reading? Why or why not? _____

✂ —

STUDENT SURVEY

Student name _____   Date _____

Parent Name _____

1. What is your favorite activity to do at school? _____

2. What is your favorite activity to do at home? _____

3. What would you like to learn more about? _____

4. If you had free time, which of the following would you choose to do? (circle one)

    read a book   draw a picture   play outside   watch TV

5. What rule do you think we need in our classroom so that everyone is treated with respect?

_____

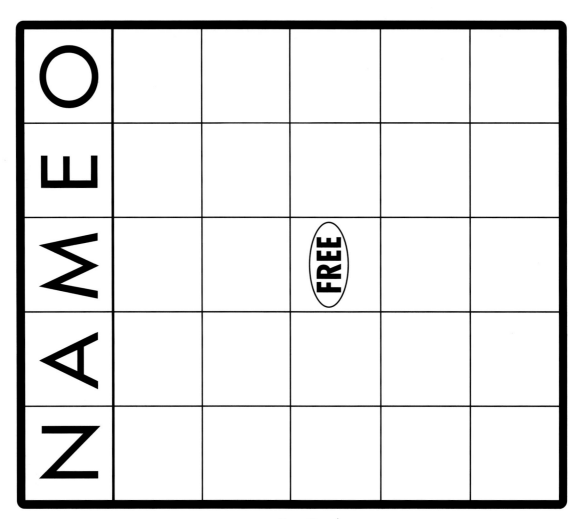

Name-O card

	A	B	C	D	E	F	G	H	I	J	K	L	M
1													
2													
3													
4													
5													
6													
7													
8													
9													

grid

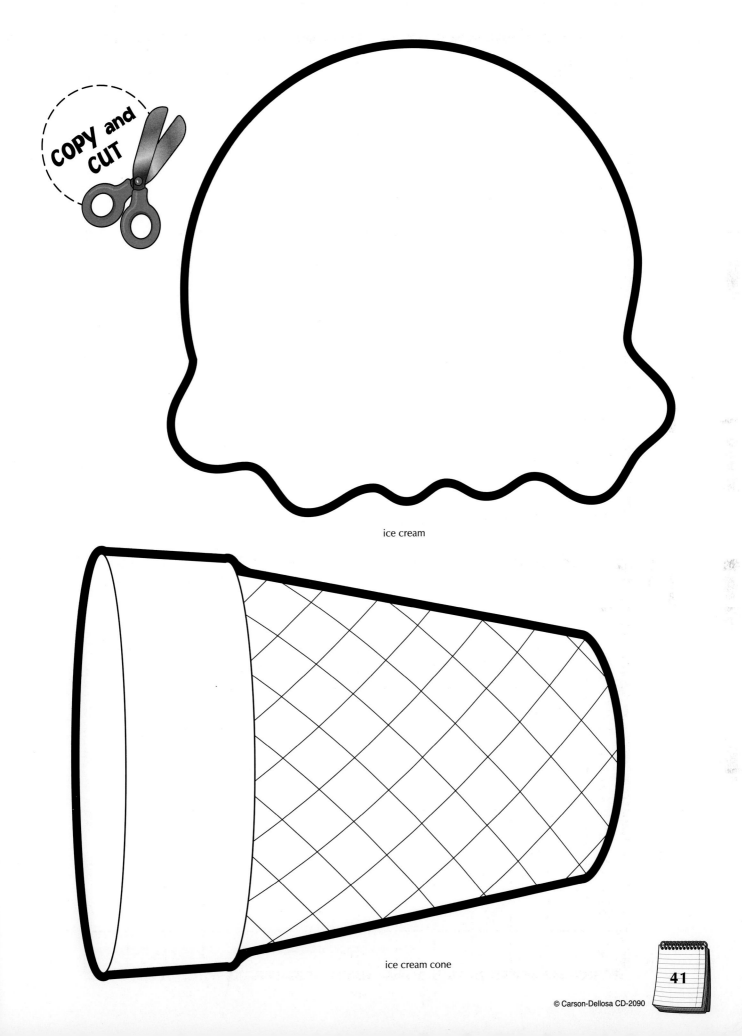

COPY and CUT

ice cream

ice cream cone

41

bus

COPY and CUT

schoolhouse

BUILDING GOOD CHARACTER

There's no time like the beginning of the school year to foster good character traits in your students—after all, Children's Good Manners Month, Courtesy Month, and Smile Week all fall in August and September! Make character education part of your everyday classroom study with these activities about manners, perseverance, self-discipline, responsibility, friendship, and that symbol of happiness everywhere, the smile!

LITERATURE SELECTIONS

The Little Engine That Could by Watty Piper: Penguin Putnum Books, 1979. (Picture book, 48 pg.) Children will learn perseverance from this classic tale about a little engine and a big mountain.

Little Red Hen by Paul Galdone: Houghton Mifflin, 1985. (Picture book, 32 pg.) Teaches the timeless lesson of gaining rewards from hard work.

A Sip of Aesop by Jane Yolen: Scholastic Trade, 1995. (Storybook, 32 pg.) Includes favorites such as "The Fox and the Grapes" and "The Tortoise and the Hare."

MIND YOUR MANNERS

MANNERS MATTER

Remind students to respect each other with these well-mannered dolls. Brainstorm a list of good classroom manners, such as *Do not interrupt when others are talking* and *Say please and thank you.* Enlarge several paper doll patterns (page 56) and have students cut them out and write the classroom manners on the dolls. Display the linked dolls with the title *Good Manners Link Us Together!*

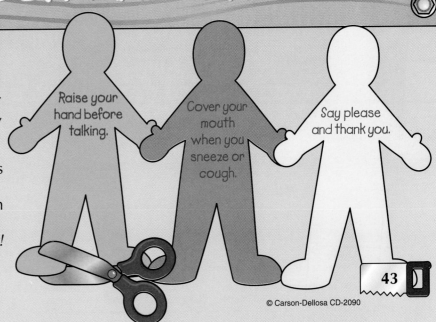

Raise your hand before talking.

Cover your mouth when you sneeze or cough.

Say please and thank you.

LUNCHTIME ETIQUETTE

Your class will have good manners "covered" with this unusual art project. Provide a large, paper tablecloth (available from party supply and grocery stores), and a lightweight paper plate and napkin for each child. Let each child draw a self-portrait on a paper plate, and glue it to the tablecloth as a reminder that they should always practice good manners. Then, let each child write a good table manner on the paper napkin and tape it below or above his self-portrait. Display the completed tablecloth on a bulletin board titled *Good Manners for Meals*.

Eat politely

Clean up spills

THUMBS UP FOR GOOD MANNERS

Maria helped Juan carry a stack of books to the library.

Give this manners game two thumbs up! Program index cards with situations that show both good manners and bad manners, or let groups of students write their own scenarios. Place the cards in a container. Allow individual students to select cards and read them aloud. Students should give a thumbs-up for each example of respect and good manners, and a thumbs-down for bad manners. For each situation that depicts bad manners, let the students think of ways they could be respectful of others and show good manners in the same situation.

A CLASS ACT

Practice makes for perfect manners. Set up a puppet theater and practice role-playing good manners. To make simple puppets, use markers, paint, and yarn to decorate upside-down, white paper cups with faces and hair. Glue a craft stick to the inside of each cup for children to hold as they "act." Post situations to act out using the puppets, or let children write their own. Once scenes have been practiced, invite parents or other classes to visit the classroom and watch the drama unfold.

PLEASE, Throw Away Your Trash

☆ Thank You

GOOD MANNERS: YOUR CIVIC DUTY

Begin a school-wide campaign for good manners. Have students complete the Always Use Good Manners! worksheet (page 53) to start students thinking about different places to use good manners. Let students come up with slogans and design posters promoting good manners. Display the posters in hallways and the lunchroom to remind everyone to use good manners.

PUBLIC SERVICE ANNOUNCEMENT

Your stars will shine in their own public service videos. Discuss how to use good manners in a variety of settings, such as the lunchroom, classroom, and on the playground and school bus. Assign a small group to each area, instructing them to write a short skit, create props, and act out their scenes. Let volunteers give an introduction and closing comments. Use a video camera to record rehearsed skits. Share the video with other classes to encourage good manners throughout the school. If a video camera is not available, take several photographs of each skit, and share a good manners photo album with other classes.

Respectfully Speaking

Teach kindness through comics with this activity. Give each child a strip of paper, approximately 12" x 4". Have students fold the papers to create four equal sections. Children can illustrate their own kindly comic strips by drawing characters in situations where kind words would be used. Have the children draw speech balloons above the characters and then trade with a partner to write respectful, kind words in each other's speech balloons. Bind the finished strips into a class kindness comic book.

Be a Class Act with Good Manners!

MANNERS BANNER

Children will not forget their manners when they see this inspirational banner! Brainstorm catchy phrases about good manners, such as *Be a Class Act with Good Manners*. Cut a piece of poster board to fit over the door to create a banner or door topper, depending upon the space available. Next, work in small groups to write and illustrate the good manners phrases using markers, crayons, or paint. Attach the illustrations to the door topper. Then, hang the banner over the outside of your door, facing out toward the hallway, to remind all visitors to remember their good manners when in your classroom.

STAR-STUDDED BEHAVIOR

Reward good manners with an all-star activity. Enlarge a class set of star patterns (page 54), plus one enlarged star pattern. Color and cut out the enlarged star and display it on a wall or door. When a child demonstrates good manners, write his name on a star pattern, along with a phrase describing his respectful behavior. Then, punch a hole in the top of the pattern and thread a length of yarn through the top of the star to create a necklace, or use a safety pin to attach the star to his shirt. For older students, attach the students' stars to a *Shining Stars* bulletin board.

45

THE CHOICE IS IN YOUR HANDS

Help students think critically to decide how to make responsible choices. Ask students what choices they've made that day. Responses might include choosing what to wear or choosing a seat on the bus. Ask students to think of a serious choice that they have made, such as studying for a test, or one they might face in the future, such as saying "no" to drugs. To complete the activity, have children trace both hands on a large sheet of construction paper and write *On one hand I could…* over the left hand, and write *On the other hand I could…* over the right hand. Inside the hands, write and illustrate two choices, one good and one poor, for addressing the issue. Complete the assignment by writing a paragraph explaining which option is better and why.

On one hand I could…

Study and do my best

A+

On the other hand I could…

Not study and get a bad grade

F

DON'T BLAME ME!

Students take responsibility for their own actions with this activity. Brainstorm a list of excuses, then come up with responsible things to say instead. For example, instead of saying, "Your toy was old anyway!," say, "I'm sorry I broke your toy. I will replace it." Write situations on slips of paper, such as, *I owe my friend an apology for something I said,* and *I got a bad grade on a test,* and put them in a bag. Let two student teams take turns avoiding excuses and being responsible in each situation. Teams earn a point each time a member has a responsible response.

DISCIPLINED DIAGRAMS

Children will write the definition for a good student with this critical thinking activity. Think about what a responsible, self-disciplined student would look like. What would he do? What materials would he have? How would he interact with the teacher and other students? Photograph students demonstrating responsible school behavior, then glue the pictures to sheets of construction paper. Turn the photographs into diagrams by drawing arrows to various parts of the photos and labeling them in question form, describing the responsible and self-disciplined behaviors. For example, draw an arrow to point out the student's feet and add a label which reads, *Do you keep your feet flat on the floor, under your desk, and to yourself?* Display the diagrams on a bulletin board to remind students of responsible, self-disciplined behavior.

Do you sit quietly and do your work?
←

Do you keep your feet flat on the floor, under your desk, and to yourself?
←

PERSEVERANCE PENNANTS

STICK TO IT!

Inspire perseverance with pennants fit for cheerleaders! Cut paper in half diagonally from corner to corner to form triangles. Write motivating messages on the pennants, such as, *Stick to it*, and *Try, try again*, and decorate with colorful designs. Glue the triangles onto pencils or craft sticks. Wave the pennants whenever a student needs extra encouragement.

OVERCOMING OBSTACLES

Make overcoming obstacles second nature! Have children complete the Be Your Best worksheet (page 52). Discuss how each child in the story overcame an obstacle. Set up an obstacle course using both physical and academic challenges for students to "hurdle," such as adding a list of numbers, building a structure of a specified height with craft sticks and clay, or jumping rope 25 times. Before completing the obstacle course, have each team create a trophy for another team, using empty soda bottles, glitter, paint, plastic cups, etc. Teams must work together to complete all tasks. Let teams that finish early cheer for others using Perseverance Pennants (above). When all teams have completed the course, present trophies for impressive perseverance!

PERSEVERANCE ☆

Dear Abby,

Let your students become advice columnists like Dear Abby! For younger students, write short letters involving dilemmas such as, *I want to be able to play the piano, but I don't like to practice. What should I do?* Older students can create their own letters. Have students write letters of advice in response suggesting how to make a responsible choice. Create a newspaper display on a bulletin board to post the questions and advice letters. Read the letters and responses aloud and vote on the best advice. Let older students read their classmates' advice letters on the board, then write letters in response to the advice, stating whether they think the advice is good and why or why not.

SHINE ON!

Put the spotlight on students with a classroom talent show. A talent show lets children show off skills they have gained through perseverance and self-discipline. Skills can range from playing an instrument to shooting baskets to subtracting two-digit numbers. Let students pick something that they have worked hard to learn. Have them write paragraphs about their skills, explaining how they have persevered and disciplined themselves to learn these skills. Invite parents, other classes, etc., to attend the talent show. Arrange the talent show so each student can read his paragraph, then perform his skill or talent. At the end of the talent show, reward every shining star with a ribbon or a small prize.

BE A FRIEND

TRAITS OF A FRIEND

What makes a true friend? Let students give examples to define the character traits of a friend. Make a chart on poster board like the one shown. Have students describe how friends show that they are fair, trustworthy, honest, and compassionate and write their responses under the appropriate headings. Display the poster during the following activities on friendship.

A Friend Is . . .

Fair
Joe and I take turns going first when we play tic-tac-toe.

Suzy lets me play with her toy car and I let her play with my doll.

Trustworthy
I can tell Shauna secrets and she won't tell anyone.

If I lend my book to Derrick, he will take care of it and return it to me after he's read it.

Honest
Drake doesn't tell me big stories that aren't true.

When Rosa wrecked my bike, she told me it was her fault.

Compassionate
Jane helped me write a get well card to my grandfather when he was sick.

Pedro visited me in the hospital when I had my tonsils taken out.

Do Unto Others As You Would Have Others Do Unto You.

A FRIEND IS FAIR

Use the golden rule to teach the value of friendship. Ask the students if they have ever heard of *The Golden Rule*. Explain that the golden rule was written a long time ago to remind people how to treat others fairly. Call on a student to recite the golden rule or recite it yourself: *Do unto others as you would have others do unto you*. Discuss what this phrase means and how it can help people remember to treat others fairly. Make golden rule reminders by writing the rule on a piece of construction paper and then drawing a thin line of glue around the phrase to frame the rule. Sprinkle the frame with gold glitter.

A FRIEND IS TRUSTWORTHY

Practice trustworthiness with a "trust walk." Take the class outside to an open area. Have pairs of students stand at one end of the area. Arrange obstacles in the area, such as cones, chairs, etc. Place a smaller object, such as a book or ball, at the other end. Instruct one partner to close his eyes. Have the other child take her partner gently by the arm and lead him to the object, using words as guides. Then, have her guide her partner in picking up the object and bringing it back to the starting point. Next, have the partners switch roles and perform the trust walk again. Discuss how children had to trust their partners to guide them safely, and that the partner had a responsibility to safely lead the other student.

48

A FRIEND IS HONEST

Use classic stories to teach classic character traits. Explain that *Aesop's Fables* have been retold for thousands of years. The morals of these animal tales offer advice and wisdom and still ring true today. *Aesop's Fables* point out the value in such characteristics as perseverance, self-discipline, and honesty. The value of honesty is found in several of Aesop's Fables including *The Boy Who Cried Wolf, Mercury and the Woodman, The Frog and the Ox, The Jackdaw and the Peacocks,* and *The Wolf and the Old Woman.* Locate a book of *Aesop's Fables* and share the stories with the class. Call on students to describe how each story relates the importance of honesty. Let each student choose his favorite fable to illustrate and write the moral of the story in his own words under his illustration.

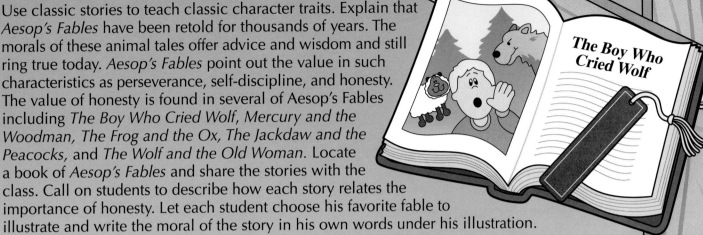

The Boy Who Cried Wolf

A FRIEND SHOWS COMPASSION

Secret pals can be good friends! Share class stories about caring and compassionate friends. Let the class draw names for secret pals. Tell students they should not reveal who their secret pals are, but should do kind and thoughtful deeds for their secret pals during the week, such as leaving them treats or kind notes, or drawing them pictures. At the end of the week, allow the children to guess who their secret pals were. Then, have students write thank-you letters to their secret pals.

To: Mindy
From: Your Secret Pal

RECIPE FOR FRIENDSHIP

With a pinch of guidance, your students can mix up a batch of friends! Brainstorm ingredients for a good friend, such as one child, a smile, an invitation to play a game, etc. Students can write the ingredients and a recipe for friendship on the index card, then decorate their completed cards. Display the cards on a bulletin board titled *Recipes for Friendship.*

A Friend
by
Yolanda McCall

Ingredients:
Me
A New Friend
A Smile
A Sunny Day
A Soccer Ball

First, I will introduce myself to the new kid. I will show her my soccer ball and ask her to play with me. Then, we will play on the playground and have a good time. I will even invite her to my house to play. We will be friends!

red   yellow

49

WANTED! A TRUE FRIEND!

THIS PERSON MUST BE:

kind, caring, fun
easy to talk to

REWARD:
A FRIEND IN RETURN!

WANTED: A FRIEND

Round up students worthy of friendship just like in the old west! Copy and enlarge Wanted Poster patterns (page 56) on manila colored paper for an old west look. Have each student trim the edges of the poster and draw a picture of a real or imagined friend in the center. Under their pictures, students can write a few positive traits of a friend. Post the completed Wanted Posters around the classroom.

COLORS OF FRIENDSHIP

Provide the following materials for each student: 8" colored yarn, one red bead, one blue bead, one green bead, one yellow bead. Direct students to tie a knot about 1" from one end of the yarn and string one bead onto the yarn. Have each student make another knot about 1" from the first knot and string another bead onto the yarn. Tell students to continue tying knots and stringing beads until all of the beads are on the yarn. Assist students as they tie the ends of the yarn together to form bracelets. Next, display the poem above on the chalkboard or poster board for students to read aloud together. Have students copy the poem on index cards to give to special friends along with their friendship bracelets. If desired, have students exchange with each other so they can keep a friendship bracelet themselves.

The Colors of Friendship

Red is for honesty, something friends always show.
Blue is because I trust you. You'll do what's right, I know.
Green is for fairness. A friend who's fair is good to find.
Yellow is for compassion, because you are so kind.
So every time you wear this, just remember that a friend
Is thinking of you dearly—I hope our friendship never ends!

Kite Schedule
Tom - Mon.
Wed.
Fri.
Jeff - Tues.
Thurs.
Sat.

FRIENDLY CONFLICT RESOLUTION

Even friends have disagreements. Students can learn how to calmly resolve their conflicts with this dramatic play activity. Reproduce the conflict resolution cards (page 55) and cut them apart. Divide the class into six groups and have each group choose one card. Allow time to discuss the conflict and decide on a solution. Call on groups to read their cards aloud and act out the conflict and resolution.

50

LOVE TO SEE YOU SMILE!

This activity is sure to result in great big grins! Begin by having the children share with the class things that make them smile, such as a playful puppy or waking up on a snowy morning. Create smiling self-portraits on paper plates using crayons and markers. Provide materials such as construction paper and yarn to make hair, shirt collars, etc. When the self-portraits are complete, have children write sentences across the bottom of the plates describing something that makes them smile. As a finishing touch, give each child a handful of dried white beans or miniature marshmallows to glue on a toothy grin!

SPECIAL DELIVERY SMILE

Use these special certificates to hand-deliver a smile to a family member or friend. To make a certificate, cut a colorful piece of poster board into 4" x 6" rectangles, or provide colorful index cards. Have children use markers to write a cheerful phrase and sign their names. Attach colorful adhesive dots (available at office supply stores) around the border of the certificate. Add smiley face features using drops of colorful glue or markers. What a way to brighten someone's day!

A PUZZLED SMILE

This puzzle will reveal…a smile, of course! Give each child 10 wooden craft sticks. Place the craft sticks on a flat surface, one above the other. Place a long piece of clear tape on the left and right sides to hold the sticks together. Draw and decorate a happy face using markers, making sure not to color over the tape. After the ink has dried, turn over the group of sticks and write a message intended to make someone smile. Have the children remove the tape and give their craft stick puzzles to a friend to solve for "double the smiles" of fun.

PICTURE PERFECT SMILE FRAME

Capture those picture perfect smiles for years to come! Make smile frames using markers and poster board. Cut a 5" x 7" rectangle from poster board. Then, draw a smaller rectangle, about 4" x 6", in the center of the larger rectangle. Cut out the smaller rectangle to create a frame. Draw happy faces and write happy phrases on the frame. Use a disposable camera to take a picture of each student. Glue the picture to the frame, then cut sections of magnetic tape to place on the back of the picture frames so they may be displayed on a refrigerator.

51

Name _____

BE YOUR BEST

Directions: In this story you will meet three children. Each child is using a different character trait to meet her goals. Can you identify which child is using which trait? At the bottom of the page, draw a line from the child to the character trait he shows in the story.

It was time for school to start. Janet almost left her homework on the school bus. She was having trouble remembering to bring her homework to school, but her teacher, Mrs. Johnson, gave her a special red folder to put her homework in. Janet has only forgotten her homework once since then. Janet took her folder to class and sat down at her desk beside a new student named Tashika. She went to school at home for kindergarten and first grade. She was still trying to get used to school rules. Mrs. Johnson started class and asked if anyone knew what special day it was. Tashika knew and wanted to call out, "The first day of fall," but she remembered that Mrs. Johnson said to raise her hand. Mrs. Johnson was happy to see Tashika raise her hand, and called on her to give the answer.

Next, Mrs. Johnson collected homework. She told Janet she was proud of her for remembering her red folder. Mrs. Johnson collected Janet's friend Andy's paper, and asked him if he was ready to recite his math facts. Andy said, "I'm ready to try again!" He had been stuck on the threes and fours multiplication tables. Tashika and Janet were already on sevens and eights, and Andy knew if he kept trying, he'd get there, too. He recited multiplication facts for three, and then for four. The next thing he knew, the whole class was clapping! He had done it! Next week he would move on to the fives and sixes multiplication tables. Everyone, including Mrs. Johnson, was very proud of him.

Janet   self-discipline

Tashika   perseverance

Andy   responsibility

Name _____

ALWAYS USE GOOD MANNERS!

Cut out the six squares at the bottom of the page. Paste each cutout square into the correct square above it, to show good classroom, playground, and lunchroom manners.

Classroom Manners   **Lunchroom Manners**   **Playground Manners**

© Carson-Dellosa CD-2090

Take turns.

Raise your hand.

Put away toys and books.

Eat politely.

Throw away your trash.

Share with others.

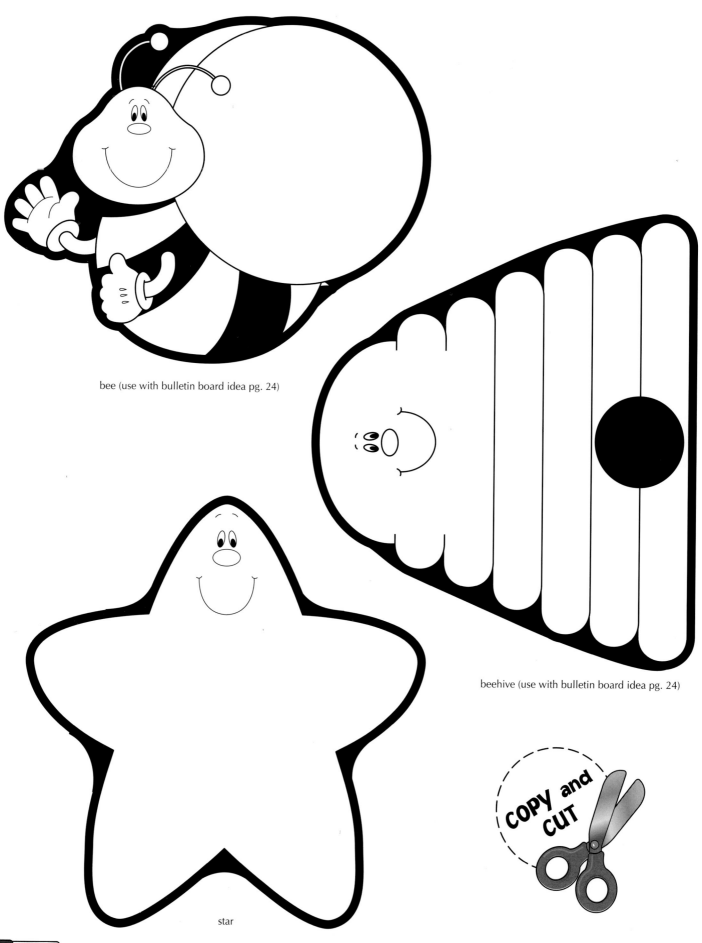

bee (use with bulletin board idea pg. 24)

beehive (use with bulletin board idea pg. 24)

star

COPY and CUT

Conflict Resolution Card #1

Ashley and Hayley are best friends who play together every day at recess. Today Molly asked Hayley to play with her at recess. Hayley really wants to play with Molly, but she doesn't want to hurt Ashley's feelings. What do you think Hayley should do?

Conflict Resolution Card #2

Victoria's friend Donisha is coming over after school. Donisha gets to ride home on the bus with Victoria! Before school is over, Donisha tells Victoria her stomach hurts and she doesn't feel like playing. Victoria is very disappointed. What do you think Victoria should do?

Conflict Resolution Card #3

Adam and Ricky ride the bus together every day. Josh is a new student who has just started riding their bus. He asks Ricky if he can sit in Adam and Ricky's seat with them. Ricky says, "No way!" What do you think Adam should do?

Conflict Resolution Card #4

Sara and Sally have known each other since preschool and they tell each other everything! One day, Sara tells Sally her parents are getting a divorce. At school that day, Sally eats lunch with her friend Mary. Do you think Sally should tell Mary about Sara's parents?

Conflict Resolution Card #5

Terry was waiting in the back of the lunch line to buy his lunch. His friend Caroline told him to come and stand in the front of the line with her. What do you think Terry should do?

Conflict Resolution Card #6

Stefan and Drew saved their money to buy a package of sports stickers to use at school. There are five sheets of stickers in the pack. Both boys want the extra sheet of stickers. What do you think they should do?

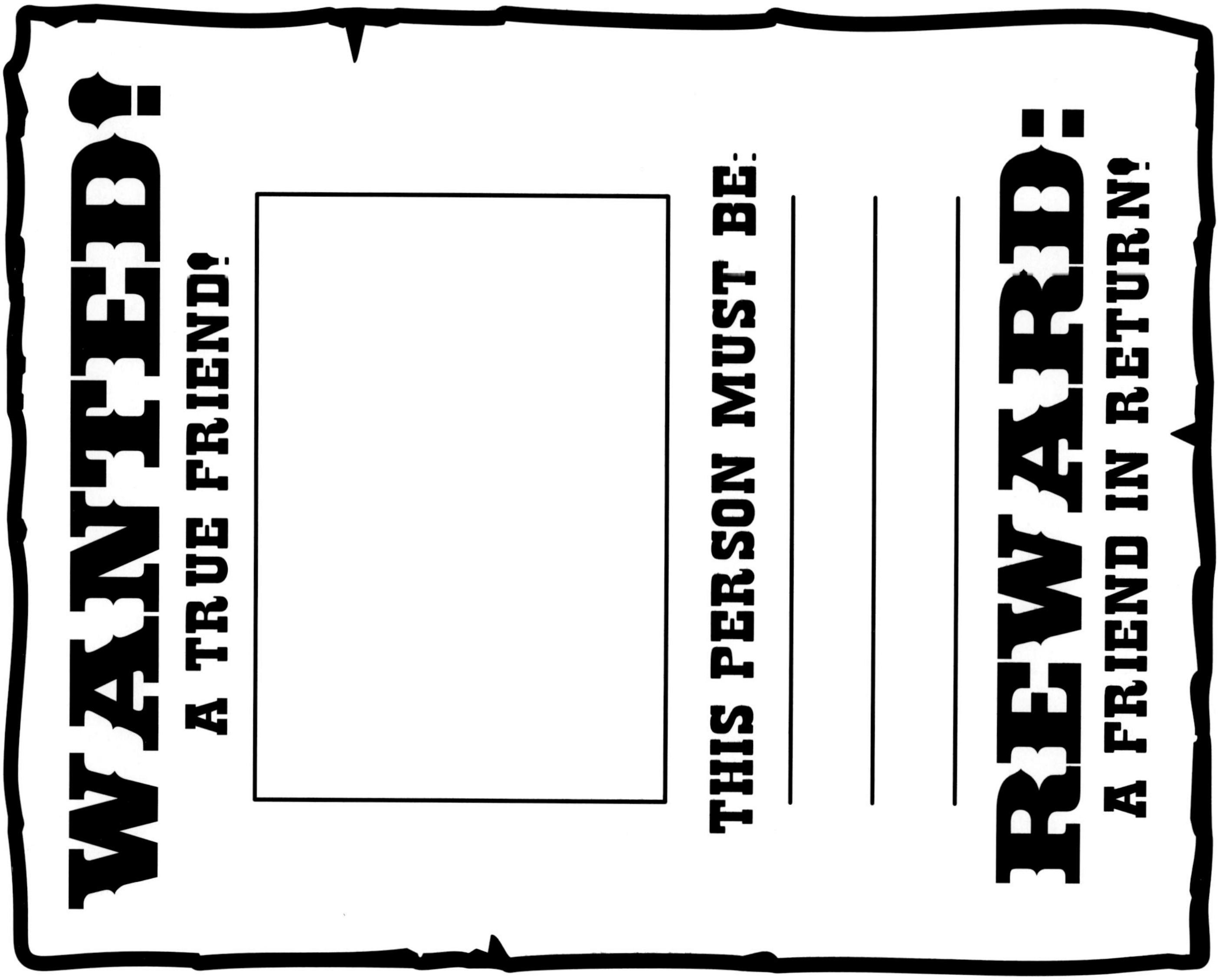

WANTED!
A TRUE FRIEND!

THIS PERSON MUST BE:

_____

_____

_____

REWARD:
A FRIEND IN RETURN!

Wanted Poster

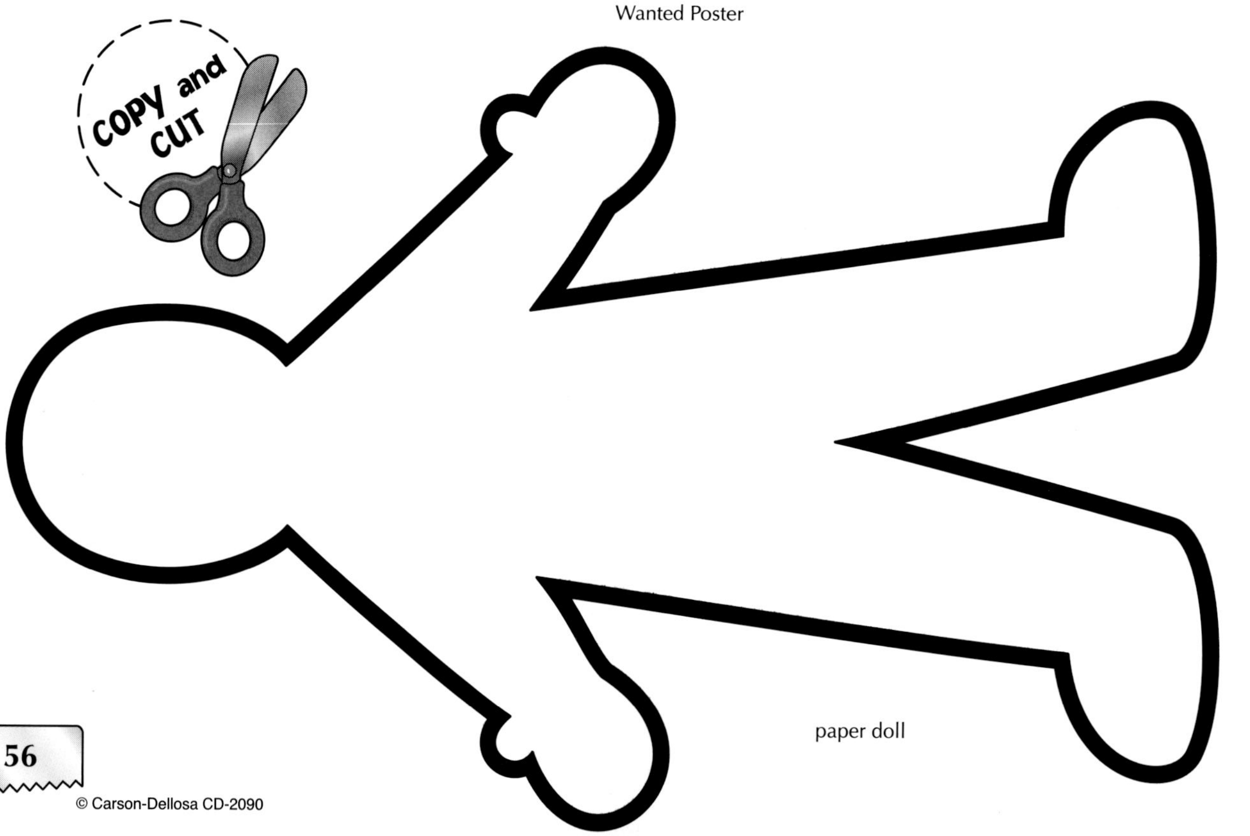

COPY and CUT

paper doll

A Bushel of Apple Fun

From their beautiful blossoms to their crisp, crunchy fruit, apples are an a-"peel"-ing classroom theme. Get your bushel baskets ready to fill with fun apple activities!

Did You Know?

- The dried bits at the bottoms of apples are the remainders of the apple blossoms.
- The Pennsylvania Dutch created the art of carving dolls from apple cores.
- Colonial people called different types of apples by descriptive names, such as *Melt-in-the-Mouth* and *Winter Banana*.
- In 1914, the Golden Delicious apple was entered in an apple contest. A contest judge liked it so much that he paid $5,000 for the tree and enclosed it in a steel, burglar-proof cage.

Literature Selections

The Apple Pie Tree by Zoe Hall: Scholastic Trade, 1996. (Picture book, 32 pg.) Two sisters anxiously wait for their apple tree to bear fruit.

Apple Picking Time by Michele Benoit Slawson: Crown, 1998. (Picture book, 32 pg.) Tells the story of a town pitching in with the fall apple harvest.

An Apple Tree Through the Year by Claudia Schnieper: Lerner Publishing Group, 1993. (Picture book, 48 pg.) Traces the life cycle of an apple tree and orchard.

Johnny Appleseed by Steven Kellogg: William Morrow & Co., 1988. (Picture book, 48 pg.) A tall tale about a true American hero!

The True Tale of Johnny Appleseed by Margaret Hodges: Holiday House, 1999. (Picture book, 32 pg.) Unusual pictures and interesting text recount John Chapman's travels from Pennsylvania to Indiana.

Apple Pickers Wanted

Have some apple-picking fun by thinking of new and unusual ways to harvest apples! Eating apples are picked by hand and placed into canvas bags to prevent bruising. The bags open at the bottom to allow apples to slide gently into larger containers. Applesauce and juice apples are harvested by a machine that shakes the trees so that the apples fall to the ground. If your students were apple pickers, what new apple-picking machines would they invent? Let them draw detailed apple-picker diagrams and label each part. Which one will work the best? If desired, display a real bushel basket full of apples to provide artistic inspiration!

57

Apples A-Blossoming!

The sweet smell and attractive color of apple blossoms make them a favorite with honeybees! As bees land on the blossoms to get nectar, they spread pollen and help the blossoms grow into apples. "Grow" apple blossoms in your classroom by enlarging several apple blossom patterns (page 62) on poster board. Cut them to make stencils. Have students trace the blossoms onto pink paper plates, then cut them out. Punch three small holes in the center of each plate, and one at the top. Thread yellow pipe cleaners into the holes and curl them to resemble the blossom's stigmas, and put one at the top for hanging. Dab perfume or scented oil on the pipe cleaners to make sweet-smelling blossoms. Draw and cut out honeybees to glue to the pipe cleaners, then hang the blossoms from the ceiling.

A Pocket Full of Apples

This handy "pocket" book will give students the scoop on how apples grow. Explain the life cycle of an apple so that children will be able to write a descriptive sentence about each stage. Fold three sheets of construction paper in half vertically, then staple the edges together to make pockets. Staple the pockets together, adding a half sheet to the front for a cover. Cut out seed shapes from brown paper, then color the blossom and apple patterns (page 62) to place in the pockets. Have the children decorate their covers and write descriptive sentences about each stage of growth on the pockets.

A Sense of Apples

Apples are a "sense-sational" food, so celebrate their taste and texture by writing sensory lantern poems. Brainstorm a list of descriptive apple words. Have each child write a lantern poem using the guidelines shown. Then, transfer the poems to decorated apple patterns (page 62). Add another apple pattern to the back, and then staple the edges together, leaving a space to stuff with cotton or crumpled newspaper. Post the 3-dimensional apples around a classroom apple tree.

Lantern Poem
Line 1—1 syllable
Line 2—2 syllables
Line 3—3 syllables
Line 4—4 syllables
Line 5—1 syllable

crunch!
bright red
sweet to taste
such a good snack
yum!

Apple-rithmatic

How do apples add up? To find out, have each child divide a sheet of white construction paper into six equal sections. Give each child a random, even number of apple seeds. In the first section, glue the seeds to the paper and write a sentence stating the number of seeds she received. Tell the child that exactly half of the seeds will produce trees. In the second section, write and illustrate the number of trees that grew from the seeds (number of seeds divided by 2 = number of trees). In the third section, draw trees again, gluing an equal number of cinnamon candies to each tree to represent apples. In the fourth section, count the apples, write the math problem (number of trees multiplied by number of apples on each tree) and answer representing the total number of apples. Then, use red paint to make the same number of thumbprint apples. In the fifth section, dip an apple half into red paint, make an apple print, draw seeds, and write a sentence telling how many seeds are in one apple. In the last section, multiply the number of seeds in one apple by the number of apples in section four, to find the total number of seeds. Let students trade papers with partners to check their answers.

① There are 6 seeds.

② $6 \div 2 = 3$ trees

③

④ $3 \times 4 = 12$

⑤ Each apple has 3 seeds.

⑥ $3 \times 12 = 36$

TRY NEW

Apple pie flavored ice cream

How about some **Apple** pie à la mode? All in one! made with real **Apple**

How 'Bout Them *Apples*?

Cakes and pies and muffins and jam—many yummy treats are made with apples. Provide food labels and boxes which list the word *apple*. Cut out only the word *apple* from each label. Have small groups each write and illustrate an advertisement featuring a delicious product made with apples, using the cutout apple word in place of the word *apple* throughout. Have each group appeal to the class by presenting its advertisement.

"A-Peeling" Treat

All this talk about apples is sure to make students hungry for a tasty apple treat! For a class of 24, provide 24 cored, peeled, chopped apples (older students can help prepare the apples with adult supervision). Follow the recipe below to make delicious homemade applesauce.

24 apples peeled, cored, and cut into chunks
Juice from 2 lemons
2 cups water
1 cup sugar
1 tablespoon cinnamon (add more to taste, if necessary)
Heat apples, lemon juice, and water in a saucepan. Stir in sugar. Boil, then reduce heat to low and cover. Cook for 30 minutes or until apples are soft. Remove mixture from stove and add cinnamon. As the mixture cools, give a cup to each student. Have them stir the mixture to make applesauce. You may wish to let children take home applesauce in plastic containers, with student-made recipe cards attached. Yum!

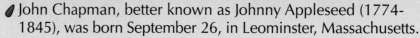

HAPPY BIRTHDAY JOHNNY APPLESEED!

Did You Know?

- John Chapman, better known as Johnny Appleseed (1774-1845), was born September 26, in Leominster, Massachusetts.
- Johnny grew apple seedlings to sell or give to settlers traveling to the Midwest.
- The apple seeds Johnny planted were gathered from cider mills after the apples were pressed.
- Johnny learned how to live off the land by traveling with Native American tribes.
- Descendants of apple trees Johnny Appleseed planted still survive across the Midwest.

Portrait Of A Special Man

Nobody knows for sure what the mysterious Johnny Appleseed looked like, but descriptions written by settlers and friends have left some clues. Children can each draw a picture of Johnny Appleseed as you read the following descriptions written by settlers and friends during his lifetime:

Johnny Appleseed was tall, thin, and had long hair and a beard.
Johnny usually wore a hat made of raccoon skin or cloth.
He carried tools, food, and apple seeds in a knapsack.
He wore whatever clothing he could find, sometimes making it from old sacks.
Johnny often did not wear shoes.

Compare the drawings with a teacher-provided drawing of Johnny Appleseed. You may wish to make your own drawing, or display one from the cover of a book about Johnny Appleseed (see page 57 for literature selections).

A Legend in Our Own Time

Traveling barefoot through snowdrifts, playing with a bear family—these are just a few legends about Johnny Appleseed! Although Johnny did travel across the Midwest planting apple seeds and surviving in the wilderness, many tall tales have been made up about his life. Let your students' imaginations run wild as they write and illustrate legends about themselves. Encourage them to take real events and rewrite them as adventure stories, complete with tall tale names. Let your young living legends share their stories aloud.

Me as Davey Birdsaver

Davey Birdsaver: This hero found a hurt baby bird. He helped the bird and it taught him to fly. They flew over mountains and trees looking for other birds that needed help, and Davey saved them all!

60

Mapping Johnny's Journey

Johnny Appleseed's travels spanned several states and many miles. Retrace Johnny's steps by giving small groups enlarged copies of the Johnny's Journey map pattern (page 62), red, washable ink pads and a few apple seeds. Cover the states Johnny visited with red thumbprints. Glue on an apple seed to mark the cities of Leominster, Massachusetts, where Johnny was born, and Fort Wayne, Indiana, the western-most point where Johnny is thought to have traveled. Have groups research what Johnny did on his travels through these states. What an incredible journey!

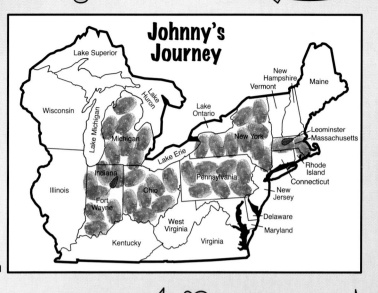

A Book of Apple Seed Memories

Help Johnny keep track of his apple seed adventures by creating individual memory books. Supply reference materials, such as encyclopedias, to use as a basis for journal entries which describe Johnny Appleseed's travels through the Allegheny Mountains, along the Ohio River, and into Indiana. Talk about the Native Americans and settlers he met, and the wildlife and plants he may have seen on his journey. Children can write and illustrate their entries on enlarged apple patterns (page 62), and then bind the patterns into a scrapbook. Let students share their books in small groups.

Sing a Song of Appleseed

Assign familiar songs, such as *Row Your Boat* or *London Bridge* to small groups, instructing them to come up with new lyrics to the songs. The lyrics must be about the life and times of Johnny Appleseed! Write down the lyrics of each song, then copy them for the class and have a Johnny Appleseed tribute sing-along. You may want to use this example to get started:

(sing to the tune of *Darling Clementine*.)
Johnny Appleseed, Johnny Appleseed.
He walked a long, long way,
To plant so many apple trees.
We enjoy them still today!

Tasty Turnovers

Celebrate the birthday of Johnny Appleseed with a treat he surely would have enjoyed! Provide cans of apple pie filling and refrigerated crescent roll or biscuit dough. Flatten a triangle of crescent roll dough on a paper plate, then add a spoonful of apple pie filling to the center. Fold over the corners and pinch them together to form a turnover. Bake according to package directions. Sing *Happy Birthday* to Johnny Appleseed with your class and enjoy the apple treats!

apple blossom
(also use with bulletin board idea pg. 25)

COPY and CUT

apple (also use with bulletin board idea pg. 25)

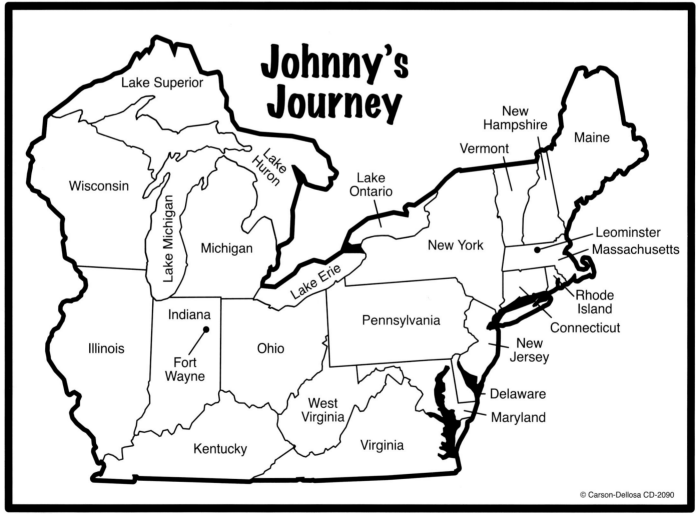

Johnny's Journey

Lake Superior

Lake Huron

Lake Ontario

New Hampshire

Vermont

Maine

Wisconsin

Lake Michigan

Michigan

New York

Leominster
Massachusetts

Indiana

Lake Erie

Ohio

Pennsylvania

Rhode Island

Connecticut

Illinois

Fort Wayne

New Jersey

Delaware

West Virginia

Maryland

Kentucky

Virginia

Johnny's Journey map

COMMUNITY COUNTS!

Whether your students live in a big, metropolitan area or a small country town, their community plays an important part in their daily lives. Explore the aspects of community life as you build a sense of belonging among your students!

Literature Selections

➡ *Come Back, Salmon: How a Group of Dedicated Kids Adopted Pigeon Creek and Brought it Back to Life* by Molly Cone: Sierra Club Juveniles, 1994. (Nonfiction book, 70 pg.) An elementary class cleans up a stream and preserves it as a salmon spawning ground.

➡ *Community Helpers From A to Z* by Bobbie Kalman: Crabtree Publishing, 1997. (Picture book, 32 pg.) This alphabet book features all kinds of people who work in a community.

Curious George Takes a Job by H. A. Rey: Houghton Mifflin, 1974. (Picture book, 48 pg.) Curious George gets a job as a window washer—with hilarious results.

Helping Out by George Ancona: Clarion Books, 1990. (Picture book, 48 pg.) Photos show kids and adults working together in various settings.

NEIGHBORHOOD ⤵

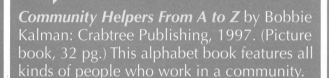

Small Town Life

Create a classroom metropolis using odds and ends. Brainstorm a list of community buildings beforehand and post it as a sign-up sheet so that each child selects a different building. Provide small boxes, such as milk cartons and cereal boxes. Cover the boxes with white bulletin board paper and let each child choose a community building to make from the box. Provide paint, crayons, markers, construction paper, scissors, glue, and fabric to turn the boxes into community buildings. Provide adhesive labels and decorate them to look like building signs, then attach them to the buildings. Tape bulletin board paper to the top of a table and arrange the labeled buildings on top. Complete the community scene by drawing streets, signs, trees, and grass. (Three-dimensional streets can be made using glue and dried beans or lasagna.) Take a classroom vote to name your tiny town!

63

Community Learning Centers

Drama is sure to unfold in these community learning centers. Set up changeable learning centers for dramatic play to represent different community places. For example, set up a restaurant center using a cafeteria tray, pretend food and cooking utensils, plates, and cups. To set up a bank, provide play money, checks, a stamp pad, pens, and paper. Other fun community places for the center could be a post office, doctor's or dentist's office, florist, and, of course, school!

All Part of a Community

Students will enjoy painting a rosy picture of their community! Explain that a community is a group of people who live (or work or attend school) in the same area. Sometimes a community is small, like a family, and sometimes, community is large, like a city. Ask the class to name types of communities of which they are members, such as class, neighborhood, etc. Divide the class into three groups and give each group a piece of butcher paper large enough to cover 1/3 of a bulletin board. The groups can draw scenes to depict a school, neighborhood, or city. Display the scenes on a bulletin board as a large community mural.

YOU ARE HERE

Find your place in the community with this map activity. Display a local map. Review directional words and symbols such as north, south, east, and west. Students can work together to place stickers or pins on the map to indicate the locations of special places such as the school, mall, etc. When students have sharpened their map-reading skills, reproduce the Community Map Worksheet (page 72) for each student to complete.

What's Happening In Our Community

Recycle recent newspapers into a community events collage. Begin by decorating a nearby hallway bulletin board or wall space in your school. Let pairs of students look through the newspapers and cut out stories of local interest. Glue the stories onto white poster board, leaving enough space to draw around them. Instruct students to add illustrations and informative captions. Provide art supplies to create letters and borders. Post the articles and illustrations in the designated space, creating a community events/news display for the entire school to see what's going on at a glance.

ABCommunity

Help your students learn the ABC's of community by having groups work together to write a list of 3-4 community locations that begin with each letter of the alphabet. For example, "A" could stand for apartments, airport, auto shop, antique shop, etc. Make several local phone books available for research. Give each group an 11" x 17" sheet of paper, and have them use markers to draw their assigned letters as large as the paper, one letter per page. They should then use the space inside and around the letter to illustrate and label the community locations that begin with that letter. Display them to create an alphabetical community reference.

Be a Tourist!

Teresa at the statue of
Otto Von Mushmouth

Spend a day as a tourist to raise awareness of the special things your community has to offer. Check with your Chamber of Commerce or Tourist Agency to borrow videos, magazines, or other information that promotes your community. Divide students into small groups, and assign each group a community tourist attraction. Let groups use the resources to learn about each tourist attraction, then create fliers about what they have learned. Gather any necessary props and clothing to become tour guides and workers for each attraction. On Tourist Day, wear tourist-type gear to class, such as sunglasses, camera, etc. The groups can role play various jobs at the tourist attraction as you walk around the room and visit the local sites. Just like any tourist, take lots of pictures at your destinations!

Our Class Works Together

Work together as a class to emphasize that having a successful classroom community requires the participation of all members. Plan a class project that requires everyone to play an important role. For example, have the class clean up the playground, and give each child a small job, such as trash bag carrier, sidewalk sweeper, can collector, etc. Time the students to see how long their project takes, then talk about how working together makes things easier—and is more fun, too!

Sign My Community Shirt!

Make all students feel like they belong with this pens-on activity. Brainstorm a few positive contributions each student makes to the class. As a class, brainstorm a list of positive classroom team names, then cast votes to choose the class name. Let students write the class name on the backs of white T-shirts with fabric paint, put on the t-shirts, and then take turns using markers to write positive contributions they have made to the class on each others' shirts. Plan to do a special class activity, such as the Our Class Works Together activity above, to commemorate this special day.

65

Good citizens help others.

What Does a Good Citizen Look Like?

Show students that good citizens look a lot like...them! Brainstorm the things good citizens do, such as vote, volunteer at a humane society, clean up garbage, etc. Assign students to groups and let them use cardboard boxes, art supplies, and butcher paper to create live-action scenes of people performing acts of good citizenship. For example, students could paint a large box to look like a voting booth, and pretend to vote in it. Photograph the children acting out the citizenship scenes. Write a caption for each photograph, such as *Good citizens help others*. Post the pictures on a bulletin board titled *This is What Good Citizens Look Like!*

Reach for a Goal

Create a show-of-hands for being a good citizen with this fun display. Give pairs of students large sheets of paper and let one partner at a time trace the other's arm. Let each child cut out the traced copy of her arm, write her name on it, and color it. Ask each student to cut out a large paper star and write a goal for making the classroom community a better place, such as *I will wait my turn to talk in class*. Make a simple banner titled *We Will Reach Our Citizenship Goals!* Glue the arms around the banner, then glue the stars just out of reach of the hands to imply reaching for a goal.

What a Citizen!

Use the *What a Citizen!* form (page 73) to encourage acts of kindness and build a caring classroom community. Set up a citizenship jar and a stack of *What a Citizen!* forms (page 73) in the classroom. When one student is kind to another, have the student who receives the act of kindness fill out a *What a Citizen!* form and put it into the jar. At the end of each week, draw a form from the jar, read it aloud to the class, and reward the special citizen with a treat. Be sure to include some slips for teacher's helpers!

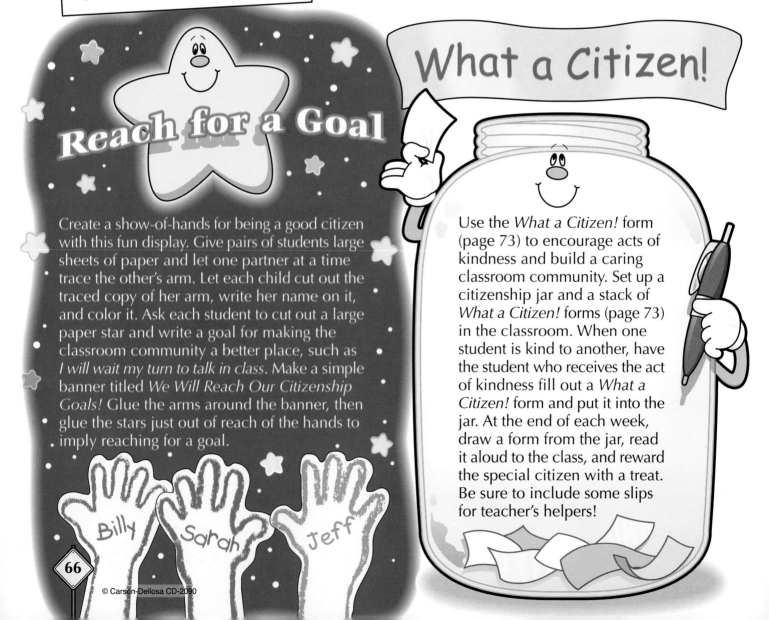

Billy   Sarah   Jeff

Oh Say Can You See What Good Citizens Are We

Being a good citizen is about more than doing good deeds. It is also about having pride in your community. Discuss the different ways that people show pride in their country, such as standing at attention for the National Anthem or flying the flag. Build pride in the classroom by dividing students into small groups and having them write a classroom community anthem. Suggest some familiar song tunes to use in their anthems. Groups can perform their anthems, then vote to choose one for the classroom anthem to sing on special occasions.

A Pyramid of Rules

The pieces of a community puzzle come together when its citizens follow the rules. Explain that following the rules in a smaller community, such as a family, is connected to following rules in a larger community, such as a neighborhood. Let the children think of home, school, and neighborhood rules they follow that are similar and make each place better. For example, children should respect parents at home, teachers at school, and neighbors in the neighborhood. Give each student a copy of the rule pyramid (page 73) and have him write and illustrate a rule, and apply it to all three places. Let students cut apart their pyramids into puzzle pieces. Have partners piece the puzzles together and review the rules shown.

Partners in Citizenship

Everybody needs a helping hand, including school staff members. At the beginning of the year, create a Good Citizens Program by matching students with staff members who wish to participate. Have students fill out Get-to-Know-Me forms (page 73) to give to their staff members. Throughout the year, designate several Citizenship Days. On these days, allow students to volunteer with their staff partners for half an hour to help with everyday tasks. For example, a student paired with a teacher could read a story to her class. Make sure to send a note to staff members a few days before each Citizenship Day so that they can prepare for their helper's arrival!

67

Spread Some Joy

Let junior citizens spread smiles and handmade flowers to senior citizens at a local retirement center. To make paper flower bouquets, provide an 11" x 18" sheet of green construction paper for each child. Fold the paper in half lengthwise, then cut 1"-wide horizontal strips in the paper, starting at the folded edge and stopping an inch from the edges. Have students roll the cut, folded paper into a tube, staple it together, and bend the paper strips down and outward. Let students trace flower patterns (page 74) onto construction paper and cut them out, then glue the flowers onto the folds of each strip to create bouquets. Arrange a day for students to visit the retirement center to present their bouquets.

① 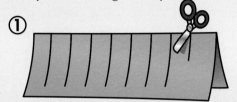 ②  ③

A Box-ful of Volunteers

Give children an opportunity to volunteer during their free time at school. Make a classroom volunteer box and fill it with in-class job slips. When a child has free time in class, allow him to select a slip from the volunteer box and perform the job. When all of the children have volunteered, reward them by volunteering to spend some class time doing a special activity with them. You may want to suggest in a note to parents that they create an at-home volunteer box as well.

Make handmade flowers for grandparents day

Ask Not What Your Community Can Do For You...

Make sure that "giving back" is a part of learning about the community. Brainstorm a list of benefits children receive from belonging to a community, such as friendship, services, and safety. Set aside a day for children to contribute something positive to the community, such as planting flowers in a park, donating used items to a shelter, contributing goods to a food drive, writing letters to the school board suggesting how to make their school better, visiting a humane society to pet the animals, etc. Let each student draw a picture of himself doing the project, and write a short paragraph about what they learned from the experience. When the activity is complete, pass out copies of the citizenship badge (page 74) for children to decorate and proudly wear.

Humane Society
I worked at the humane society on Saturday helping with the rabies clinic. We helped make sure that dogs and cats were safe. I gave out bones to dogs after they got their shots. I like dogs.

Curtis Phelps

City Park
I helped plant five new trees at the city park garden. The trees will grow into new homes for squirrels and birds. One day maybe they will be big enough to climb on and play under.

Jane Thomas

68

CAREERS ⤵

Get to Know the People in Your Neighborhood!

Let's meet the people in your neighborhood! Raise students' community helper awareness by explaining that different jobs provide different kinds of services to the community. Post four large sheets of chart paper on a bulletin board and write a category from the lists below on each sheet. Before the activity, write the names of different community jobs on sentence strips, and place them in a career-related hat or other container. Take turns pulling a job out of the hat, reading the name aloud, and taping it under the appropriate category. After all of the sentence strips have been posted, write additional jobs on sentence strips and add them to the list. Keep the list posted while the class studies community helpers.

Jobs Helping People

mail carrier
doctor
teacher
firefighter
police officer

Jobs Selling Things

baker
butcher
florist
realtor
jeweler

Jobs Helping Nature/Animals

veterinarian
park ranger
gardener
zookeeper
landscaper

Jobs Building/ Fixing Things

plumber
architect
carpenter
repair person
electrician

BIG BOOK
Of Community Careers

This class big book is sure to be bustling with community activity. Have each child choose a community career to be featured as part of the class community book. Cut large pages from poster board about the height and width of a grocery bag and give one to each child. Instruct her to illustrate her community helper and label the picture with the community helper's job title and a sentence describing what the helper does. Glue the pieces of poster board to each other back-to-back. Reinforce the sides of the pages with masking tape. Bind the finished pages to create a class community book.

69

Tools of the Trade

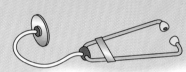

Students will learn the tools of many trades with this hands-on activity. Start with a discussion about tools used in different careers, such as a doctor's or nurse's stethoscope, plumber's wrench, baker's rolling pin, etc. Gather as many tools as possible and place them in a large box. Let students take turns choosing an object from the box and acting out the career that utilizes the tool, while the rest of the class guesses the career. For an extra challenge, include some tools which could be used in several careers, such as a calculator, ruler, or computer keyboard, and act out only one career as the class tries to guess.

THIS CAREER IS CLASSIFIED

CLASSIFIEDS-JOBS

Community careers won't remain a mystery for long when students investigate real world job examples. Provide several copies of classified job advertisements from newspapers. Let each child choose a career that sounds interesting to him, list positive aspects of the career, then rewrite the advertisement with a twist—he can't name the career. (Instruct him to write the name of the career on the back of his ad.) Collect the advertisements and then post them on a "job wall" to see if other children can guess the careers being described.

The BEST Person for the Job

Wanted: Teacher
· Loves kids
· Likes to have fun
· Smart
· Likes school
· Likes to read

Let students "apply" their best writing skills to find out what they want to do for a living! Explain that people often choose careers based on their talents and what they like to do. Mention a few careers and brainstorm necessary skills for each one. Then, let each child choose a career to write about, listing the skills and type of person needed for each job. Post all of the descriptions and let each child choose a job. Have each student write a job application comprised of several sentences explaining why her skills would make her a good candidate. Post all of the applications around the job descriptions.

70

Firefighter

Community Faces

Children can see themselves in a variety of careers with these creative displays. Cut several sheets of poster board into 11" x 17" rectangles, then cut several large circles from shiny silver wrapping paper, aluminum foil, or other reflective material. Glue each shiny circle near the top of each piece of poster board. Divide the class into groups, then assign each group a community helper. Give them an enlarged corresponding hat pattern (pages 74-75) to color and cut out, then paste above the reflective circles. Display the finished signs on a chalkboard tray so that children can stand in front of the shiny circles and "reflect" on the many possible career choices they have before them!

Career Connection

They are all connected—careers, that is! Explain that many careers are connected and depend on each other to be successful in helping the community. Choose a career and write the title and its description on an index card. Attach the career to a ribbon or streamer, leaving the long end of the streamer hanging at the bottom. Ask if anyone can think of a career that is affected by the one you have written on the card. For example, if you have written *farmer* on a card, then *baker* is affected by *farmer* because the baker needs wheat from the farmer to make bread. Write *baker* on another card and attach it to the streamer under the first card. Additional cards on this streamer could be *grocer, restaurant owner, chef, waiter,* etc. Make several career connection streamers and hang them from the ceiling in your classroom. You may wish to let the children illustrate each career listed.

Farmer grows wheat

Baker uses wheat to bake bread

Grocer buys bread to sell

Restaurant buys bread to serve

THANKS For All You Do

Choose a special day near the Labor Day holiday to show community workers how much they are appreciated. Explain that Labor Day, the first Monday in September, celebrates the working people who make communities a better place. Help thank workers by making thank you pins. Give each child a 4"-diameter circle cut from poster board, and provide washable ink stamp pads in a variety of colors. Make thumbprints on the circles using many colors of ink. Add happy face features to the thumbprints using fine-point markers, then use permanent markers to write thank-you messages on the circles. Glue a safety pin to the back of each circle, and let children present their pins to community helpers as a special "thank you."

71

© Carson-Dellosa CD-2090

Name _____

Community Map Worksheet

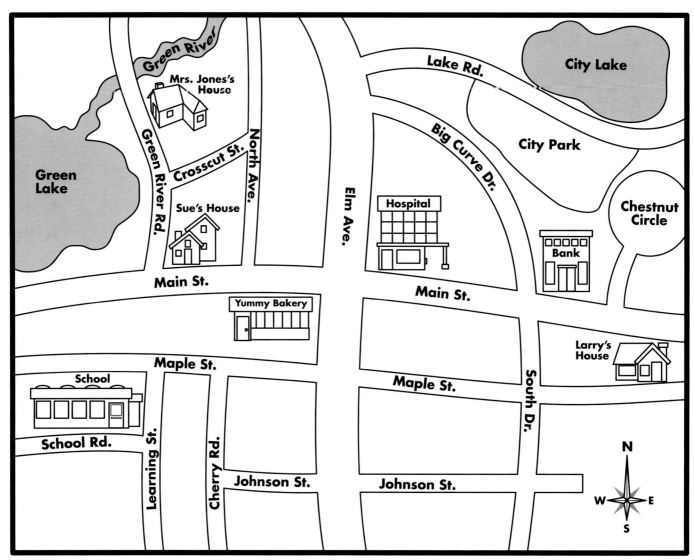

1. Does Larry live in the east or west part of the community? _____

2. How many blocks does Larry have to travel to get to school? _____

3. What is the name of the community bakery? _____

4. On what street does Mrs. Jones live? _____

5. How many lakes are in the community? _____

6. Should Sue travel north, south, east, or west to get to the bank? _____

7. The community hospital is on the corner of _____ Street and _____ Avenue.

WHAT A CITIZEN!

_____

is a great citizen because

_____
_____
_____
_____
_____
_____

SIGNED

Get to Know Me

1. My name is _____ .
2. My teacher is _____ .
3. I am in the _____ grade.
4. I am here because

_____
_____
_____
_____ .

GOOD CITIZENS HELPING OTHERS

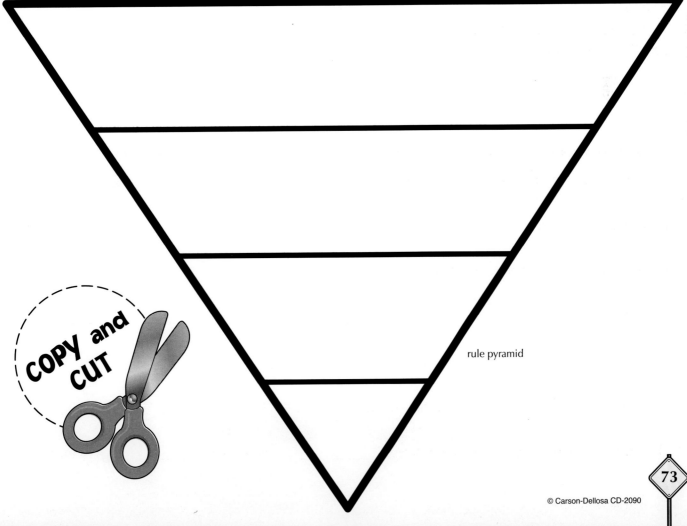

rule pyramid

COPY and CUT

citizenship badge

flower

flower

COPY and CUT

flower

FD 7

firefighter's hat

police officer's hat

WHAT A CITIZEN!

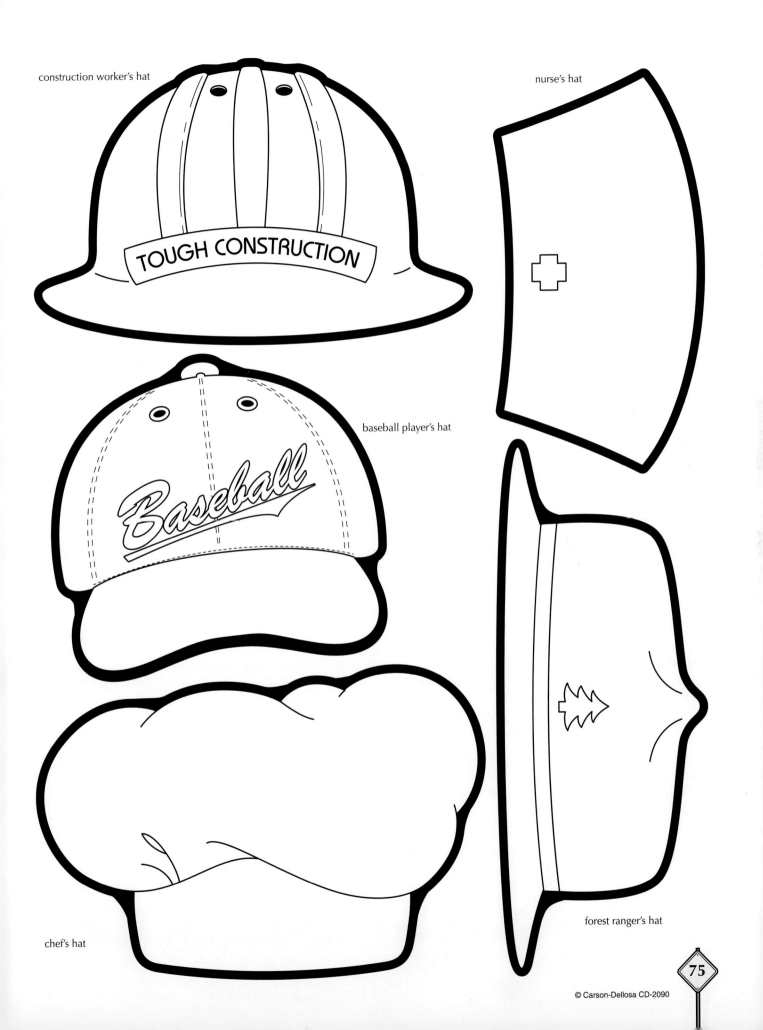

construction worker's hat

nurse's hat

TOUGH CONSTRUCTION

baseball player's hat

Baseball

chef's hat

forest ranger's hat

75

© Carson-Dellosa CD-2090

National Hispanic Heritage Month

During the weeks between September 15 and October 15, Hispanics and other Americans celebrate National Hispanic Heritage Month. The celebration starts at 11:00 p.m. on September 15th, when Mexicans begin celebrating their Independence Day.

Did You Know?

Anyone with ancestors from Spain, Mexico, Puerto Rico, Cuba, Central, or South America is considered to be of Hispanic origin. The exception to this is Brazil, which was settled by the Portuguese.

Hispanic Heritage Week was first celebrated in the United States in 1968. In 1988, Congress changed the Hispanic Heritage celebration from one week to one month.

Hispanic Heritage month recognizes all of the contributions Hispanics have given to American culture, including language, cuisine, and citizens. Today in the United States, about 26 million citizens are of Hispanic Heritage—about 10% of the US population!

Literature List

The Adventures of Sugar and Junior by Angela Shelf Medearis: Holiday House, 1995. (Picture book, 32 pg.) Junior Ramirez and Sugar Johnson share the same apartment building. By the end of the story they also share ice cream, a monster movie, and a close friendship.

America is Her Name by Luis J. Rodriguez: Curbstone Press, 1998. (Picture book, 32 pg.) America is a Hispanic girl who moves to the country for which she is named, and finds she is homesick.

In My Family/En Mi Familia by Carmen Lomas Garza: Children's Book Press, 1996. (Picture book, 32 pg.) Using vibrant paintings, the author describes her life as a Hispanic girl in a Texas border town.

Amazing New Sites

Many places and landmarks in North America were seen by Spanish explorers before anyone else from Europe! Mount a large map of North America on a bulletin board. Write the names of the Spanish explorers below, and the corresponding information listed below on a set of index cards, and let small groups match the places on the cards to their correct map locations. If possible, attach photographs of some of the objects and places (Grand Canyon, buffalo, Mississippi River, etc.) to the backs of the index cards.

Hernando de Soto In 1541, was the first European to see the Mississippi River.

Juan Ponce de Leon In 1513, first European explorer to see Florida and claim it for Spain. Also tried to discover the Fountain of Youth.

Francisco de Coronado First European to see the Grand Canyon in Arizona during a 1540 expedition.

Alvar Nunez Cabeza de Vaca Probably the first Spanish explorer to see buffalo, in about 1536, somewhere between Mexico and California.

Vasco Nunez de Balboa First European to see the Pacific Ocean, in 1513 at the isthmus of Panama.

Pedro Menendez de Aviles In 1565, founded what is now the oldest city in the United States: St. Augustine, Florida.

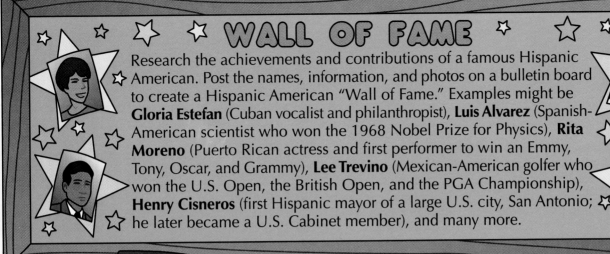

WALL OF FAME

Research the achievements and contributions of a famous Hispanic American. Post the names, information, and photos on a bulletin board to create a Hispanic American "Wall of Fame." Examples might be **Gloria Estefan** (Cuban vocalist and philanthropist), **Luis Alvarez** (Spanish-American scientist who won the 1968 Nobel Prize for Physics), **Rita Moreno** (Puerto Rican actress and first performer to win an Emmy, Tony, Oscar, and Grammy), **Lee Trevino** (Mexican-American golfer who won the U.S. Open, the British Open, and the PGA Championship), **Henry Cisneros** (first Hispanic mayor of a large U.S. city, San Antonio; he later became a U.S. Cabinet member), and many more.

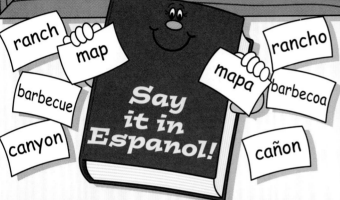

ranch map rancho mapa barbecue barbecoa canyon cañon

Say it in Espanol!

Many English words have Spanish origins, or are spelled and pronounced the same way in both languages. Divide the class into small groups. Assign each group a list of English words with Spanish origins, such as *armadillo, banana, barbecue (barbecoa), canyon (cañon), chocolate, map (mapa), patio, ranch (rancho), rodeo, tomato, tornado,* and, of course, *taco*. Use a Spanish-English dictionary to look up the words in English. Write the corresponding Spanish spellings and pronunciations on index cards (some of the words may be pronounced the same in both languages while others are spelled or pronounced differently). Let students take turns saying Spanish words to see if anyone can guess the English equivalent.

¡Viva La Fiesta! Celebrate Hispanic heritage with a class party! Provide Latin or Spanish food. Check the ethnic section of your grocery store for interesting choices, such as guava nectar, cinnamon-flavored tortilla chips, guacamole, Mexican hot chocolate, etc. Let children try their luck at smashing a candy-filled piñata. Play Latin or Spanish music and let the children dance with their maracas and bongos.

Bongos y Maracas

Make these fun (and noisy!) crafts designed to find a Latin rhythm. *Bongos* and *maracas* are traditional Latin percussion instruments. *Bongos* are drums, played by striking the skin, or vellum, with the hands. *Maracas* are made from dried gourds filled with dried beans. Provide cardboard canisters with plastic lids in a variety of sizes (potato chip cannisters, drink mix containers, and coffee cans work well). Allow each student to decorate a canister with paint, glitter, and beads. When the canisters are dry, put on the lids, then beat the lids like drums. These are the bongos. Play one bongo at a time to hear the different sounds. Then, fill the bongos with dried beans. These are the maracas. Shake the maracas to hear the different sounds. Finally, play some Latin or Spanish music, and let the children keep time with a maraca or a bongo.

77

Grandparents Day

Did You Know?

- Many countries celebrate Grandparents Day, including Australia, Canada, and the United States. The American version of Grandparents Day originated in 1973 by Marian McQuade of Oak Hill, West Virginia, as a way to honor the elderly. In 1978, President Carter declared the first Sunday after Labor Day to be National Grandparents Day. Some countries, like Japan, celebrate a Senior Citizens Day (September 15) to honor all elderly people.

- There may be children without grandparents in your class. Most of the activities in this chapter can be modified, letting children celebrate with other senior family members, friends, or neighbors.

Literature Selections

Abuela by Arthur Dorros: Penguin, 1997. (Picture book, English or Spanish, 40 pg.) A young girl imagines she is soaring over the city—with her Spanish-speaking grandmother along for the ride!

Grandfather's Journey by Alan Say: Houghton Mifflin, 1993. (Picture book, 32 pages) A boy and his grandfather explore their Japanese and American heritage.

Nana Upstairs and Nana Downstairs by Tomie dePaola: Penguin, 1998. (Picture book, 32 pg.) With the death of his great-grandmother, four-year-old Tommy learns that loved ones are always with us in memories.

The Song and Dance Man by Karen Ackerman: Alfred A. Knopf, 1992 (Picture book, 32 pg.) Grandpa cannot resist donning his vaudeville props and clothing and performing songs and dances for his three grandchildren.

My Grandparents Are Here!

Bring the generations closer together by inviting grandparents to share a day in their grandchild's classroom. On the designated day, let each child introduce her grandparents. Provide refrigerator cookie dough, waxed paper, rolling pins, and large cookie cutters for grandparents and grandchildren to make cookies together. After the cookies are baked, decorate the cookies. Make sure you photograph the activity! For children who have grandparents that live far away, invite their parents in to help make the cookies. Let the children write notes explaining what they are doing, and send the notes and photos home with parents to mail to the grandparents. Parents may wish to mail the cookies as well! You may also want to send an extra care package of any remaining cookies to an elder care facility.

When I Was Your Age...

Grandparents and other elderly friends and family can be a window to the past for children. Brainstorm a list of questions children would like to ask their grandparents about their childhood. Questions might be: *What was your favorite toy or book when you were my age? How did you celebrate your birthday? What did you want to be when you grew up?* Write the questions on a sheet of paper, then duplicate it for children to use while conducting grandparent interviews. Share answers with the class.

Nana and Grampy and Pops and Gramma!!

Ask each child to draw a picture of her grandparents on half of a large sheet of paper. Then, let each child write the names she calls her grandparents vertically down the other side of the paper (you may have some creative spellings!). Each child can then make an acrostic poem using the letters in her grandparents' names. Make a book cover from a grocery bag, and write the title *Our Grandparents* on the cover in permanent marker. Pass the book cover around and write all the grandparents' names on it. Bind the book together with yarn or ring binders. Share the completed book during storytime.

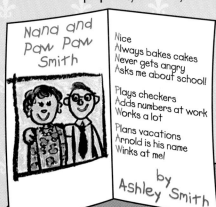

Nana and Paw Paw Smith

Nice
Always bakes cakes
Never gets angry
Asks me about school!

Plays checkers
Adds numbers at work
Works a lot

Plans vacations
Arnold is his name
Winks at me!

by Ashley Smith

Sing a Song of Grandparents

Children love to sing songs, and grandparents will be delighted to hear this one! Before you teach children the words, explain what it means to respect your elders, and to perform kind deeds.

sing to the tune of

Twinkle Twinkle Little Star

Grandparents deserve respect
So kind words we must select.
Thoughtful in each word and deed,
Loving comfort that we need!
Helping, sharing, caring, true,
Grandparents we all love you!

Special Grandparent Memories

Help create keepsake boxes to hold special things that remind grandparents of their grandchildren. Provide shoe boxes and have children bring in recent grandparent photographs from home. Let children decorate shoe boxes with paint, glitter, sequins, etc. When the paint is dry, use a craft knife to cut out a square in the center of each painted lid. Let each child tape his picture to the inside of the box lid so that the picture shows through the square.

Have children write short notes to their grandparents, explaining that the box is a keepsake box to hold special things that remind them of their grandchildren. Grandchildren may wish to place artwork or pictures of themselves and their grandparents inside the boxes.

Where Are My Grandparents?

Teach simple geography by sharing where children's grandparents live. Have each child write a short note to mail to her grandparents, asking what it is like there, what they do there, etc. (You may want to get the grandchildren to write and ask for advice at the same time, to complete the activity below.) Provide a large city, state or province, and country map (and a world map, if you have international students). Post the maps on a bulletin board. Let each child read her letter to the class. Place a push pin on the map locations named in the letters. When all the grandparents are located on the map, find out whose grandparents live farthest away, live nearby, etc.

Grandparents Give Grand Advice

Discuss the word *advice*, giving examples such as: *Don't talk to strangers, The best things in life are free,* etc. Explain that grandparents and other elderly people sometimes offer good advice because they have seen and done so many things. Have each student ask a grandparent to give him some good advice, then write the advice on a sentence strip. Post the strips on a bulletin board titled *Grandparents Give Grand Advice!*

All Kinds of Grandparents

This activity will work well even for children without grandparents. Provide a large piece of poster board and old magazines. Let the children find pictures of grandparents (with or without other family members) and paste them to the poster board. Display the poster board and let children bring in snapshots of their own grandparents. Title the display *Grandparents Are Special People!*

80

ANIMALS ON THE MOVE

Pack your bags and get your students' minds moving into the fascinating, mysterious world of migrating animals! Through the air, over land, and in the sea, animals are constantly looking for ample food and better weather. Follow their journeys and just try to keep up with these animals on the move!

Ready, Set, Migrate!

Did You Know?

- The main reasons animals migrate are to find food and a good place to raise their young.

- Changes in temperature, in length of daylight, and in their bodies tell animals that it is time to migrate.

- Animals find their way using stars, the Sun, the Earth's magnetic field, landmarks, sounds, and smells.

Literature Selections

Home at Last: A Song of Migration by April Pulley Sayre: Henry Holt & Co, 1998. (Reference book, 40 pg.) Details the migration of a variety of animals.

Monarch Butterfly by Gail Gibbons: Holiday House, 1991. (Reference book, 32 pg.) Explains the life cycle of the monarch butterfly, including how to raise one at home.

The Serengeti Migration: Africa's Animals on the Move by Lisa Lindblad: Hyperion Press, 1994. (Reference book, 40 pg.) Stunning photography accents the story of migration in the Serengeti National Park.

They Swim the Seas: The Mystery of Animal Migration by Seymour Simon: Browndeer Press, 1998. (Picture book, 40 pg.) Aquatic animals migrate through the water-color drawings of this text.

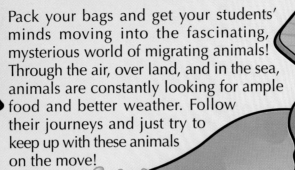

Inquiring Humans Want to Know!

Give your class of reporters this wild assignment and get the facts on migration straight from the animal's mouth. Display question words (who, what, when, where, why, how) on a poster. Let each student choose a migrating animal to interview about its journey. Have students write interview questions about migration using each question word, then have them research the answers. Each student can divide a piece of paper into six panels, then draw a comic strip in each panel, complete with speech balloons, showing herself as a reporter interviewing the animal.

81

A Tale of Two Habitats

Show "the best of times" for both of an animal's habitats. Fold a 12" x 18" sheet of white construction paper in half lengthwise. Cut a slit in the center of one side of the paper from the edge to the fold, making two "liftable" flaps. Let each student choose a migrating animal, research its summer and winter habitats, and draw a picture of a habitat on the front of each flap. Under the summer flap, have the student list what resources the animal enjoys. Repeat for the winter flap. Attach an 8" string to the back of the habitat paper. Cut out a small picture of the animal and attach it to the end of the string, so that the children can move the animal in order to view it in front of either habitat.

Magnetic Migration

North, south, east, west—how do animals know which way to go? Scientists believe migrating animals such as sea turtles and butterflies (see pages 83 and 88-9), use the Earth's magnetic fields to "pull" them in the right direction. To demonstrate this principle, reproduce small sea turtle patterns (page 92) and small maps of North America, including the Atlantic Ocean. Glue the maps to open file folders. Have small groups cut out and color each turtle and glue it to a magnet. Have one child in each group hold up a map and press a larger magnet on the back of the map behind an Atlantic beach (turtle nesting site). A second child should place a turtle magnet on the front of the map over the Atlantic Ocean, then move the turtle magnet on the paper slowly toward the larger magnet. Let each child take a turn trying to steer the turtle away from the magnet, and noticing how the magnetic force pulls it back. Encourage children to think about how magnetic forces might help steer animals in the right direction.

Serengeti Song

Every year during the rainy season, 3 million African wildebeests, zebras, and antelopes migrate in a loop from Tanzania's Serengeti National Park to Masai Mara in Kenya, in search of fresh grasses. Read to students about the amazing trek and then have them write very short stories, poems, or even songs about the mass migration. Let students write their verses or sentences across blank zebra patterns (page 91) to look like stripes. Trace over the writing with a black pen. Let the students glue their zebras to tan or green construction paper. Add paper-fringed grass, blue paper skies, and cotton ball clouds. Use markers to color the clouds gray and stormy.

Salmon Scents

Challenge your students to use their sense of smell to find their way home! Salmon are born in streams and then swim out to sea to live. At egg-laying time, they return to the same streams in which they were born. Scientists believe that salmon use their sense of smell to determine the right stream. Cut several large, stream-like shapes from blue butcher paper and place them on the floor around the room. Divide students into small groups, and give each group a small container of flavored extract, such as lemon, vanilla, or cinnamon. Ask the groups to smell and memorize the scent and then have them leave the room. Place several unmarked containers of the same spice onto each "stream." See how long it takes students to smell their way to the right streams! For fun, rearrange the scents overnight, and see if the groups still remember them the following day.

LEMON

Cinnamon

Vanilla

Turtle Travel

Open these sea creature crafts to find a tale of migrating turtles. Sea turtles, many of which are endangered, migrate for miles to lay eggs on the same beaches where they were born. When the babies hatch, they must make their way back to the sea, avoiding such dangers as birds and crabs. To make fact-filled turtles, give each child two small paper plates and one sheet of sea turtle parts patterns (page 92) copied onto green construction paper. Have each student glue the head, feet, and tail around the inside edges of a plate, then glue torn pieces of green and brown construction paper to the bottom of the same plate to look like a shell. Place the plates together so that the bottoms are on the outside, and staple them together below the tail. Give each child a white paper circle approximately the diameter of the inside flat section of a plate, and have her write facts about turtle migration on the paper. Facts might include: *Baby sea turtles eat sargassum weed when they first reach the ocean*, *Sea turtles may use the earth's magnetic fields to locate the beaches where they were born*, and *Both male and female turtles migrate when it is time to lay eggs*. Glue the circle to the inside of the bottom plate. Finally, cover a table with tan butcher paper. Place the sea turtles on top as if they are nesting on the beach, and let children open each others' turtles to read the migratory facts.

Baby sea turtles eat sargassum weed when they first reach the ocean. Both male and female turtles migrate when it is time to lay eggs.

A WHALE OF A TRIP

Your students will enjoy a chance to sail the ocean blue as they learn about whale migration! Whales are challenging animals for scientists to track because they are often underwater and not very visible without tracking devices. Use this chapter about whales to help you and your students do some whale watching of your own!

Did You Know?

- Migrating whales travel through the day and night for as long as several months at a time.

- The warm waters of the equator do not foster much whale food, so migrating whales often do not feed in these areas. They survive using the energy they have stored in their blubber.

- The gray whale has the longest migration route of any mammal. It travels approximately 6,000 miles from Alaska to Mexico.

Think Like a Scientist!

As your class begins studying whale migration, challenge them to use the scientific method and think like marine biologists! Scientists track migrating whales to see where they go each year. List the scientific method for students: think of a question, collect data, form a hypothesis, perform an experiment, and analyze the results. Ask students to consider the question: Why do whales migrate? Have each child write a hypothesis to answer this question. Then, reveal Fact #1 from the list at right. Keep revealing new facts in the order shown until the last fact is revealed. Have students revise their hypotheses according to each new fact. Which young scientist's hypotheses are correct?

Whale Fact List: Why Do Whales Migrate?

Fact #1: Whales leave the Arctic or Antarctic and travel to the equator in the fall, and return to cold waters in the summer.

Fact #2: Whales have their babies in winter and nurse them.

Fact #3: Cold ocean waters have lots of krill and plankton (tiny shrimp and sea creatures that whales eat), while the warm water near the equator does not.

Fact #4: Baby whales do not have a thick layer of blubber when they are born.

Answer: Whales migrate to warm waters to have babies, then migrate back to cold waters to feed.

A Meal Fit for a Whale

Some whales eat up to four tons a day. Krill is about the size of an adult's fingertip, so imagine how many tiny krill it would take to feed a whale! Many migrating whales do not have teeth, so how do they eat? Baleen whales have plates made of material similar to fingernails and hair. To eat, they take in large quantities of sea water, and then use their tongues to force the water out through the plates, leaving a harvest of krill and plankton trapped inside to swallow. To recreate this "straining" method of eating, divide students into small groups. Pass out combs, foam packing chips cut into pieces, and shallow pans filled with about 2" of water. Let each group stand its comb in the water, teeth down, about 1" away from the edge of the pan, and then tilt the pan toward the comb so that the water flows through the comb but the foam gets trapped. See which "whale" can collect the most "krill" at one time.

What a Fluke!

How do migrating whales travel? Unlike fish, whose tails move from side to side, whales have flukes (tail fins), which push up and down through the water to propel them forward. To demonstrate the difference, play "tail tag" with your class. Give each child a fluke pattern (page 91), and a wide strip of white paper stapled to fit a child's head. The children can color and cut out the fluke patterns and then staple them– either vertically like a fluke or horizontally like a fish–to their headbands. Designate 4-5 children to go fishing. Have the fish and whales run from one end of the playground to the other while the fishermen try to tag them. If the fishermen catch only fish, they can go fishing again. But, if they catch any whales, they must become either whales or fish. Have children trade tails after each run across the playground to keep the fishermen guessing!

Which Whale Has My Tail?

Could you spot your own fingerprint in a crowd of other fingerprints? Just like fingerprints, each whale's fluke is individually marked. Scientists use the markings on whales' flukes to recognize and track individual whales—even after they have not seen them for many days. Give out copies of the fluke pattern (page 91), and black crayons. Challenge each student to come up with a pattern that will be unique to her fluke. Write students' names on the backs of their flukes. After school, post all of the flukes on a bulletin board. As students arrive the next morning, have them attempt to identify their flukes from memory. To extend the activity, have children pretend they are scientists tracking the migratory journey of a particular whale, and write short tracking journals to post next to their flukes.

85

BIRDS OF A FEATHER MIGRATE TOGETHER!

Show your class that migration is really for the birds! While children may not see whales or sea turtles migrate, many children have spotted flocks of geese flying overhead, or noticed a change in the types of birds at the backyard birdfeeder, and will be able to relate these experiences with each other.

Bird's-Eye View

Like humans, birds often use landmarks, such as buildings, mountains, rivers, etc., to guide them to their summer and winter nesting sites. Ask children to name some of the landmarks they recognize on the way to school, such as street signs and buildings. Let each child pick a secret "nesting site" in the classroom, hide her nest pattern (page 91) there, and then draw a bird's-eye view map (looking down) of the classroom. She should label any landmarks and indicate where her nest is. Challenge your "birds" to trade maps and find each other's nests!

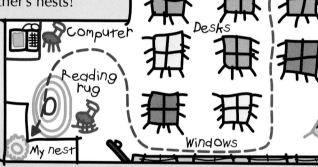

Road Runner

Migrating birds follow "highways" in the sky called *flyways*. The four flyways, labeled the Atlantic, Pacific, Mississippi, and Central, are named for the part of the North American continent they are near (the Mississippi flyway follows the Mississippi River into Canada). Show the flyways illustration and talk about what geographical features a bird might see along each flyway, such as the Pacific coastline or Central Plains. Ask students to plan how they would help a bird follow one of the flyways if the bird had to drive along the path instead of fly. Give road maps to four small groups (one per flyway) and have them write directions for a road trip following the same path. Have groups trade directions and see if they can find their way using a different flyway map. Younger students can write the direction in which the birds will drive, and what states and provinces they would pass through along the way.

86

Give Me a "V"!

Students will flock together to play this follow-the-leader game. Geese fly in a v-formation to prevent them from getting tired. The leader protects the other birds from the full force of the wind. When a leader gets tired, he flies to the back of the formation and another bird takes his place. Race car drivers and bicycle racers use the same strategy when they follow closely behind the leader of a race. Put your students into a v-formation on the playground, and have the "flock" run across the playground. Let each child have a turn leading the flock. Then, ask children if it was harder or easier to run in the front, and why. If it isn't easier to run in the back, why might it still be easier to fly behind another goose?

Flap Your Wings!

Use these bird puppets to create flocks, demonstrate v-formations, or just to have flying fun in your classroom. Make a construction paper copy of the bird and wings patterns (page 91) for each child. Children should decorate their birds, then tape the wings and bird patterns to each other. Assist children in taping one piece of yarn to the middle of the wings, then taping a 12" piece of yarn to the bottom of each wing. Tie the yarn together under the bird. Let children fly their birds around the classroom by holding the top piece of yarn and pulling gently on the two bottom pieces of yarn to make the wings flap.

Befriend Our Feathered Friends

Birds face many dangers as they migrate, such as predators, pollution, and even glass windows! Make decals to protect birds from flying into windows. Start by drawing simple bird patterns, taping them to each child's desktop, then taping waxed paper over the patterns. Have students outline the patterns with colored glue (add tempera paint to white glue for an opaque color or food coloring for a translucent color). Fill in the outline with glue. Let children add details with colored glue, if desired, and allow to dry completely. Peel off the dry glue and stick the bird decals to large windows in your school to deter wayward fliers.

These Bags Are for the Birds

Students will pack their bags (for birds, that is) to prepare for a migratory adventure! Draw and cut out pictures from magazines of whimsical things a bird might need to migrate south or north, such as sunglasses, or a baby blanket. Let students glue their pictures on suitcase patterns (page 92). Have students trade suitcases and identify which are for traveling north or south.

87

© Carson-Dellosa CD-2090

FLIGHT OF THE BUTTERFLIES

Take your class on an amazing butterfly journey! In autumn, the fragile monarch butterfly flies south from the United States and Canada to escape cold weather and find food. monarch butterflies spend the winter in colonies in Mexico and California. Toward the end of winter, monarchs return to their northern homes.

Did You Know?

- No other insect migrates as far as the monarch butterfly.

- One autumn day, two boys tagged a monarch butterfly in Minnesota. The butterfly was found by a scientist in Mexico—proof that some monarchs fly all the way across the United States to Mexico to spend the winter.

- As monarchs arrive in a winter resting place in Mexico, they spiral in large towers above the area. Some scientists believe they may be signalling incoming butterflies as to where the colony is.

Garden of Butterflies

Paper butterflies will create a cluster of color in your classroom. Some monarch butterflies migrate to a small region in Mexico, where millions gather in the middle of tree trunks to avoid wind and predators. Give each child several butterfly patterns (page 92) copied onto orange construction paper. Have each student decorate one wing with black paint, then fold it in half and press the painted portion to create a symmetrical design. Cut out the butterflies. On butcher paper, let students draw a large tree. Tape all the butterflies to the center of the tree, then let students cut out flowers in shades of red, yellow, orange, pink, and purple (monarch favorites) to attach around the tree so that the "butterflies" can have a snack! Use the board as a butterfly center to display butterfly facts and crafts.

Take a Taste...with Your Feet!

Sink your feet into some tasty stories! Female monarch butterflies use their feet to taste the plants they step on, only laying eggs on the milkweed plant. Let students write stories about tasting with their feet. What would walking be like? How would eating lunch in the school cafeteria be different? What utensils would they use? Encourage students to read their tasty tales to the class.

The Circle of Life

Recreate the butterfly life cycle in your classroom by having students follow the steps below to illustrate it on an 8" circle of poster board. Have each student draw a "+" on his circles to divide it into four sections. Next, draw a milkweed plant (the only plant monarch caterpillars will eat) in the first three sections. You may want to have older children label the sections of their drawings.

In section 1, dot the milkweed plant with glue to represent a butterfly egg.

In section 2, use markers to color a piece of tube-shaped pasta to look like a caterpillar, then glue it to the milkweed plant.

Color section 4 to look like a sky, then color shell pasta to look like a monarch butterfly and add it to the section.

In section 3, color a piece of tube-shaped pasta to resemble a chrysalis, then glue it to the milkweed plant.

Butterfly Tag

Where are you going, butterfly? No one was certain where monarch butterflies went when they migrated until a Canadian scientist adhered harmless tags to butterfly wings so that he could find them when they arrived at their southern destinations. The tags contained information about the experiment and asked the finder to record and send information to the scientist. Many butterflies were found in Mexico, so the scientist travelled there, and found many of the tagged butterflies—some from as far away as Canada! Have a class butterfly hunt commemorating the scientist's efforts. Give each child a butterfly pattern (page 92) to decorate. Have children attach labels with their names and classroom number on the butterflies' wings. Have children create *Have You Found A Butterfly?* "fliers" to place around the school, instructing lucky finders to return the butterflies to the classroom, including information about where each butterfly was found, on what day, and at what time. After school, hide all of the butterflies around the school (include a few extras in case some butterflies do not survive migration), and let your young butterfly scientists record the finders' information on a chart. Display the chart with your *Garden of Butterflies* (page 88).

Have you found a butterfly?

Johnny smith age 6
Mr. Jones class

Take It from Someone Who Knows

Amazingly, monarch butterflies are born knowing when and where to migrate—they don't need lessons! Even so, butterflies face many dangers along the way, like cold weather, predators, cars—even people who like to catch butterflies! Have the class pretend to be butterfly parents writing letters to their children, offering good advice on how to stay safe during migration. Let the class decorate stationery (a butterfly-shaped rubber stamp would work well) on which to write their letters, then post them around the room for butterflies to "see" as they fly by.

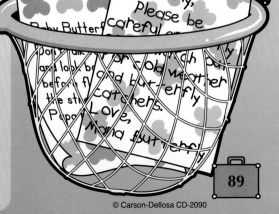

Dear Little Butterfly, Please be careful...

89

Butterfly Facts

Create high-flying books to let students show their knowledge about the majestic monarch butterfly! Give students three butterfly patterns (page 92) to cut out. Younger children will need only two. Have the children stack the patterns on top of each other, then staple them together in the center to form a center binding. Children can fold up the wings and write facts and opinions about butterfly migration on the bottom two sets of wings (not on the cover). Finally, provide cotton swabs for the children to use to paint a butterfly cover, adding black, accordion-folded construction paper for antennae. Display these books around the room and watch knowledge about butterflies take flight!

Butterfly Fun Fest!

Your class will be all a-flutter with excitement as they plan for a classroom butterfly festival. Each fall, thousands of monarch butterflies migrate to Pacific Grove, California. Pacific Grove, also known as Butterfly Town, USA, holds an annual parade to celebrate the arrival of the butterflies. To celebrate along with Pacific Grove, let your class make and enjoy these special butterfly snacks!

Wiggly Wobbly Butterflies

These yummy butterflies are as much fun to make as they are to eat! Follow the instructions on a package of orange-flavored gelatin. Spray a baking dish with vegetable oil, then pour the gelatin mixture into the baking dish and refrigerate until firm. Use butterfly-shaped cookie cutters to cut out a butterfly for each child. Decorate the wings with candy dots and use licorice as antennae.

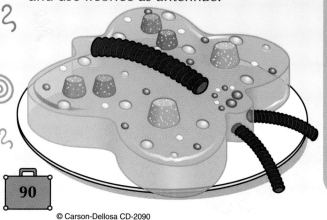

Wildflower Nectar Cups

Your children will feel like butterflies as they drink from these pretty flower cups. Pass out paper cups, along with two strips of paper (one green and one another color) to wrap around each cup. Let children cut the top edge of the colorful paper strip into petal shapes then glue it around the bottom of the cup. The green strip should be cut into a fringe, like grass, then glue the grass strip around the flower strip. Each child can then fill her cup with nectar (fruit juice). Make sure you provide your young butterflies with drinking straws—every butterfly needs a proboscis!

wings

bird

fluke

nest

zebra

COPY and CUT

91

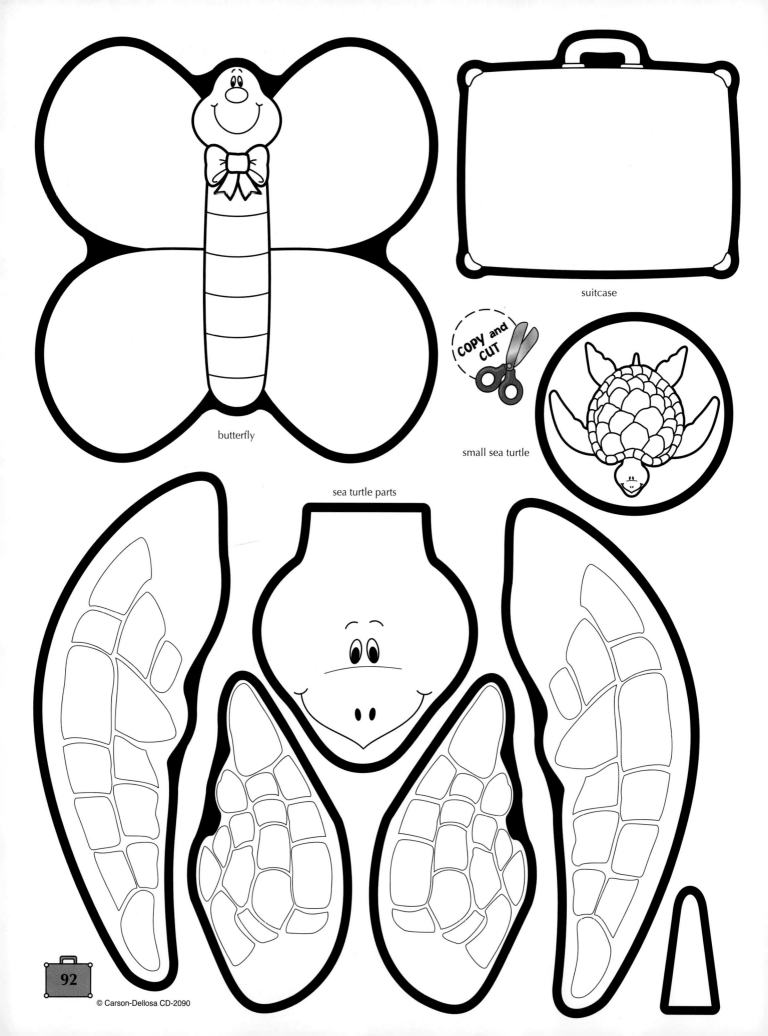

butterfly

suitcase

COPY and CUT

small sea turtle

sea turtle parts

92

© Carson-Dellosa CD-2090

INTERNATIONAL Holidays

Raksha Bandhan

This festival, celebrated every August in India according to the Hindu calendar, honors the bond between brother and sister. The name Raksha Bandhan (ROCK•sha BOND•an) literally means "Protection Bond;" *Raksha* means *protection* and *Bandhan* means *bond*. On this day, the sister ties a *rakhi*, a bracelet made of woven threads, around her brother's wrist. In exchange, the brother gives her a gift and promises to protect her.

Marks of Success

Students will not fail to have a great time when making these success symbols! During Raksha Bandhan, sisters draw *tilaks*, symbols of success, on their brothers' foreheads with tumeric powder. Have students make their own symbols of success or encouragement. Provide construction paper, markers, crayons, beads, glitter, scraps of cloth, glue, etc. Have students draw their symbols on construction paper and then decorate them. Once the symbols are completed, punch holes in the tops of the symbols. Provide each student with a 2' length of yarn to thread through the hole. Tie the ends of the yarn together and have students wear their symbols as necklaces or tied around their heads as they present them to the class.

The Ties That Bind

Students will be tied up with fun when making these bracelets! During Raksha Bandhan, sisters tie rakhis around their brothers' wrists because they believe these bracelets will ensure peace and good health for the wearer. Celebrate by making rakhis with the class. Provide 2" construction paper shapes such as circles, squares, etc., in different colors. Allow each student to pick a shape. Then, provide markers, colored pencils, wrapping paper, scraps of cloth, glitter, glue, etc. Allow the students to decorate their shapes any way they like. Once the shapes are decorated, provide several different colors of string or thin raffia. Allow the students to pick a few colors of string and braid them together. Punch a hole on either side of the construction paper shape. Thread the braided string ends through each hole and tie them together, leaving enough string so that the rakhi will fit around a wrist. Encourage students to give their rakhis to a brother or other close family member.

Raksha Bandhan (continued)

What I Like About You

Ask students to think about the qualities they like in their siblings. Give each student a piece of construction paper, crayons, markers, etc. Have students draw pictures of their siblings and write the things they like about them underneath. Encourage students to think of as many good qualities as possible. If a student does not have siblings, have him draw a picture of the siblings he would like to have and write the qualities he would like each one to possess underneath. Ask students to share their pictures with their families.

This is my sister Angie.

he is neat because she can blay the piano. By Robin

Baby Brother

I like Mitchell because he makes me smile.

by Josh

Gifts from the Heart

Have students honor their siblings or other important family members with a gift. Give each student two pieces of construction paper. Have students decorate one piece of construction paper like a wrapped gift. On the other piece of paper, have each student draw a gift she would like to give to her sibling or other family member. After the gift is drawn, staple the drawing of the gift to the back of the decorated paper. Encourage students to give the "gifts" to family members.

A Promising Letter

Since Raksha Bandhan celebrates the love between siblings, have each student write a letter to a brother or sister. The letter could contain a promise or a note of thanks. Students without siblings can write letters to family members or friends who are like siblings. After the letters are complete, let students decorate them. Encourage students to hand deliver their letters to their siblings.

Dear Brother,
You are a great big brother. I like the way you help me with my homework. My frien think you are really too. I promise to be th best little sister that I can be to you.
❀❀ Love, Shania

Rosh Hashanah

One of the High Holy Days in the Jewish religion is Rosh Hashanah (Rosh ha•SHA•na), the Jewish New Year. This holiday usually occurs in September and is celebrated for one or two days. It is a time for self-examination and remembrance as well as happiness and joy. Jews usually attend synagogues and eat foods symbolic of sweetness, blessings, and abundance. To mark the beginning of the High Holy Days, the shofar, a wind instrument made from a ram's horn, is blown in the synagogue or temple.

Make a Shofar

Not only is the shofar used to announce important events, but in Biblical times, it was also a Jewish musical instrument. Provide each student with a 9" x 11" piece of heavy brown paper or cardboard. Beginning at one corner, roll the paper so it resembles a funnel. Tape down the end. Spread glue over the outside of the funnel and wrap it with brown yarn or twine. After the glue dries, allow students to celebrate by sounding their shofars!

Heads Not Tails

During Rosh Hashanah, it is customary to have a meal which consists of either fish or a fish head. The fish head is a symbol of being on the top, or being successful (head), instead of on the bottom, or failing (tail). Provide construction paper fish shapes for each student. Provide markers, stickers, etc., and have students decorate their fish. Next, provide wiggly eyes to glue onto the fish. Give students paper plates and have them glue their fish to the plates and write a New Year's message, such as *May your merits multiply* or *L'shanah tovah*, the common Rosh Hashanah greeting. Punch a hole in the top of the plate and tie with yarn for hanging.

A Sweet Treat

Many Jews eat sweet foods during Rosh Hashanah in hopes that the coming year will be filled with blessings. Honey is usually served with apples and Challah (yeast-leavened bread). During Rosh Hashanah, the Challah is rounded instead of braided as a symbol of hope that the coming year will be smooth and not filled with unhappiness or sorrow. Bring in a rounded loaf of bread and honey and allow the students to indulge in this sweet tradition, or bring in frozen bread dough and allow students to mold their own mini-Challah bread.

L'shanah tovah

HONEY

Yom Kippur

Yom Kippur (Yom kee•POOR), The Day of Atonement, is the most sacred Holy Day in the Jewish calendar and occurs in the early fall. Yom Kippur is known as the Sabbath of Sabbaths and Jews refrain from working and fast from sunset until dark the next day in order to concentrate more fully on their prayers. On this day, it is customary to wear white and attend the synagogue for special services. The themes of the services focus on self-reflection and repentance for the individual and the community. At the end of the fast, families enjoy a special meal. The end of Yom Kippur is signified when the shofar is blown at the synagogue.

Being Good Like We Should

Yom Kippur is an appropriate time to think of good deeds. Have students make paper doll accordion booklets, complete with the good deeds they will perform. Provide each student with a paper doll pattern (page 56) cut from construction paper, and a piece of 11" x 17" paper. Have students accordion fold the paper and trace the paper doll pattern so that the arms and legs touch the folds. Cut around the shape, not cutting the fold. Have students write their names on the first paper doll, and good deeds they will do on the other shapes. Let students share their good deed booklets with the class.

Shofar Magnets

Let students celebrate Yom Kippur by making shofar magnets. Provide each student with a cone-shaped corn snack. Give each student a small magnet to glue to the back of the corn snack. You may want to spray the magnets with shellac to make them last longer. Let students take their shofar magnets home to share with their families.

It's Wise to Apologize

Yom Kippur is a day to think about who has been hurt by our words or actions and to say "I'm sorry." Have students make apology cards in honor of this holiday. Give each student a piece of construction paper folded lengthwise. Provide markers, wrapping paper, glue, cloth scraps, etc., and allow students to decorate their cards and write special messages inside. Encourage students to apologize to people they have wronged by giving them the completed cards.